The People and the Police

The People and the Police

by Algernon D. Black

Former Chairman of the New York
Civilian Complaint Review Board
and a Leader of The Society for Ethical Culture

GREENWOOD PRESS, PUBLISHERS
WESTPORT, CONNECTICUT

Library of Congress Cataloging in Publication Data

Black, Algernon David, 1900-
The people and the police.

Reprint of the ed. published by McGraw-Hill, New York.
Bibliography: p.
1. New York (City)--Police. 2. New York (City)--Police--Complaints against. I. Title.
[HV8148.N5B5 1976] 363.2'09747'1 75-40991
ISBN 0-8371-8699-4

Originally published in 1968 by McGraw-Hill Book Company, New York

Reprinted with the permission of McGraw-Hill Book Company

Reprinted in 1976 by Greenwood Press
A division of Congressional Information Service, Inc.
88 Post Road West, Westport, Connecticut 06881

Library of Congress catalog card number 75-40991
ISBN 0-8371-8699-4

Printed in the United States of America

10 9 8 7 6 5 4 3 2

Preface

This book grows out of the author's experience as chairman of the Civilian Complaint Review Board of the Police Department of New York City. The Board was established in July 1966 and was abolished by majority vote in the Referendum of November 1966. Now that it is a thing of the past, it may be appropriate and helpful for the people and the police to know some of the facts and understand the method of its organization and operation, its strengths and weaknesses.

This Review Board was unusual in that it was mixed, with police officers and a majority of civilian members. The experience and the agency were unique also in that the Board had to function in the midst of racial disturbances and stormy political controversy. Increasing crime, race riots, and protest movements presented special difficulties to the police.

The cases in this book have been chosen to illustrate the types of grievances to be found among the people. All the cases represent actual complaints made to the Civilian Complaint Review Board. In order to preserve anonymity no case is presented in its entirety.

It is the purpose of this book to bring about better

understanding and cooperation between the people and the police. It should make clear some of the problems of reviewing police performance, and it should give some perspective on civilian performance.

The problems of civilian complaints and how to deal with them are not confined to the complaints against the police. Wherever, in any branches of government, public officials or employees exercise authority for or with or over the lives of civilians there may be a movement to assure "review." Hopefully, there may be lessons in the Civilian Complaint Review Board experience which may be useful in the future in clarifying the development of the "Ombudsman" as an integral part of the processes of a democratic society.

Acknowledgments

I want to express my appreciation to those who by their generous help have made this book possible. First, I would thank my friend, Harold Baer, Jr., attorney, former executive director of the Civilian Complaint Review Board, for his encouraging support and critical examination of sections of the first draft.

Special thanks are due to my wife, Elinor Black, to my son Jonathan Black, and to Mrs. Gay James, for their invaluable and painstaking contribution to the editing of the manuscript, and to Mrs. Donna Fetonte for her devoted technical assistance in preparing the manuscript. For whatever errors or questionable statements or conclusions this book contains, the author alone is responsible.

Finally, appreciation is hereby expressed to John V. Lindsay, Mayor of the City of New York, and to Police Commissioner Howard R. Leary, for their social vision and independence and courage in bringing into being a review board on which civilians and police officers could work together in dealing with civilian complaints.

This book, with whatever usefulness it may contain,

is dedicated to the mutual understanding and mutual support between the people and the police. May it help assure to all men a greater freedom with equal justice under law.

Contents

Introduction

In 1941 a delegation from the City-Wide Citizens' Committee on Harlem walked up the steps of Police Headquarters in New York City to meet with Commissioner Lewis Valentine. Leaders from the various religious and ethnic and nationality groups of the city, clergy, tradeunionists, educators, state assemblymen, and city councilmen were all represented.

As co-chairman of the City-Wide Committee I explained why we had asked for the meeting. A few days before, a young Negro had been shot to death in the street. Early that morning he had felt disturbed and confused, and at his request his father had called for an ambulance. The young man had collected his personal laundry and was going across the street when the ambulance arrived. The young white rookie policeman riding the ambulance called out, "Does Roy Mills live here?"

"*I'm* Roy Mills," answered the young man.

"Come with me!" ordered the policeman.

"I will, Officer, I just want to take this laundry across the street."

"You come now!" the policeman commanded.

"I won't be but a minute," said the young man.

As he walked into the street, the policeman said, "You're coming with me now." He grabbed the young man's arm. The youth pulled away. The policeman, nervous, scared, and angry, drew his gun. "Come back or I'll shoot!" The youth kept walking with his laundry. The policeman shot. A patrol car turned into the block. Police jumped out with their guns drawn. The young man lay dead in the street.

We had come to protest the senseless and tragic use of the gun, the needless killing. Also, we had come to protest the commonly accepted practice of the "third degree," the beating of people in the precinct station houses of Harlem.

After a number of the delegation had spoken, Police Commissioner Valentine cleared his throat and spoke with deliberation. "Gentlemen," he said, "there are seventeen thousand policemen patrolling the streets of this great city. It would be wonderful if a little angel were perched on the shoulder of each patrolman telling him exactly what to do. But there isn't."

In July 1966, almost twenty-five years later to the day, I walked through City Hall Park in the early morning to meet with the Mayor and the members of the newly appointed Civilian Complaint Review Board. I had been asked to act as its chairman.

Since I had a few minutes to spare, I stopped to rest. Nearby a man was reading a newspaper. I said, "Do you mind if I ask you a personal question?"

He looked me over and said, "No. Just so it isn't *too* personal."

"What do you think about this idea of a review board to receive civilian complaints and to consist of civilians and police?"

The stranger spoke quickly and with assurance. "You see, I'm an accountant," he said. "I believe that an inside audit isn't enough. It's always good to have an outside audit alongside of the inside audit. Does that answer your question?"

It was time for me to leave. I walked across the park and up the steps of City Hall to meet my fellow members of the Review Board.

The Policeman's Job

People who have different jobs in an age of specialization have a hard time understanding one another. The lawyer, doctor, artist, and research worker all live in different worlds. So it is with the farmer, teacher, factory worker—and the police.

The young rookie coming out of school or factory, out of the Army or the Marines, is rarin' to go. He is proud of his uniform. He represents the government and the law. He has great hopes. Just as the young lawyer believes that there are worlds of injustice to conquer and the doctor is bent on lessening pain and saving life, so the young patrolman wants to catch all the criminals and break up the evil and lawlessness that threaten the community. He is honest and ready for hard work and danger. He may do more than the job requires. But as time passes he comes to recognize that the lawless activities of burglary and robbery, the petty thievery and gambling, the rapes and homicides, the never-ending quarrels between families and neighbors and people in the street have been a part of human life for a long time and will be around for a long time to come. He begins to accept evil as part of the reality he lives with. He loses his impetuous zeal to clean it all up. "Why knock yourself out? You can't win. Relax! Take it easy! Do the job but don't kill yourself. Why so hot and why in such a hurry, copper?"

No group is so exposed to the seaminess of human life. The more a young man is brought up in a good family and good school, and the more he has been nurtured by a good religious education and a good community, the harder it is for him to "take" the exposure. For the police are exposed to the ultimate in human foolishness, human madness, human crookedness, and cruelty. There is not a behavior which men have thought of in their worst moments that the police officer has not had to face. He sees the trickiness, the perversions, the greed and lust and sadism, the cold indifference and the ruthlessness—the corrupters and the corrupted. Inevitably, it takes its toll in the loss of sensitivity and compassion and faith.

It was evident to me one day when an individual expressed a reaction with much emotion. "You call upon people to have faith in man," he said. "That's the craziest idea I've ever heard."

"What do you do?" I asked.

He answered, "I'm a policeman."

"That explains it," I said. "You see people at their worst. You see them in the streets and when they're in trouble, when they're in a fight, or have broken the law."

"Don't kid yourself," he said. "The people I see in the streets and in trouble are the same people who just a little while before that were in their nice homes and not involved in trouble. You can't fool me. I see people in the raw, the way they really are. Underneath their fine, civilized manners and clothes they're animals."

Perhaps for most of the police there was a time when they still believed that there was good in every man and that it was possible to reach the good. But for many the experience weakens and undermines that faith. The result is a tough shield, a protective cynicism. Perhaps it is necessary to survival on the job. The thin-skinned cannot stand it. The only way is to develop a capacity to "take anything, anything that comes, and not let it get under your skin or bother you. If you expect too much of people, if you trust or depend upon them, you may fail on the job and you may even lose your life."

This need to develop a defense against the physical and psychological hazards of police work helps drive the police into a close and united fraternity. Their unique danger and difficulty make them blood brothers. Daily they all face the same kinds of difficult and dangerous situations. They all carry a gun, and by so doing they are all called to danger and the possibility of injury and death. Their lives are on the line. Their blood may be on the pavement any day.

To most people the police job is that of law enforcement. We live in a period when homicide, rape, burglary, robbery, and arson take a heavy toll of life and property and constitute a menace in every community. We count on the police to protect life and property, to prevent lawlessness, and to apprehend the lawbreaker. We expect the police to have the strength, skill, and courage to deal with the criminal offender no matter how desperate and dangerous he may be. Indeed, we count on the police to cope with the crime problem even where it is tied in with organized gambling and the rackets in narcotics, liquor, and other commodities and services—even where crime is protected by hired thugs, shrewd lawyers, and connections with the corrupt parts of the business community and the crime syndicates and political machines. Organized crime is a lucrative big business and pays off and protects its own. Against this powerful, ruthless antisocial reality the police have to bring to bear their top-level criminal investigative talents and their utmost courage. These are some of the more obvious and dramatic aspects of police work.

At times youth presents special problems to the police. Whether it be vandalism or petty offenses or serious delinquencies, the public expects the police to act with firmness and also with understanding. But the "youth problem" takes on serious proportions and requires police action when a massing of frivolous college youth turns an after-game rally into a lawless riot which disrupts the local community and endangers life and property. Police have to take on the leather-jacketed motorcycle gangs traveling through the community thirsting for trouble, committing vandalism, and provoking conflict with local youth. So, too, the police have a special responsibility and difficult task when gang warfare threatens between black and white or Puerto Rican and Italian youth in the streets of the city. Here again the job is a delicate one requiring firmness, restraint, impartiality, and judgment.

Since every district of a large city presents different conditions and problems, no one uniform police directive or practice can meet all the needs of the entire city. The precinct police center or "station house" located near the docks, railroad yards, and warehouses must deal with the special problems deriving from the water front: ship arrivals and departures, longshoremen conflicts, foreign seamen, and the highjacking of trucks and merchandise. In the precinct house located in Greenwich Village the police briefings may cover the handling of extreme nonconformists, the problems presented by offbeat centers, narcotics, the coffeehouses, "hippies," and Washington Square Park at night and on weekends. This precinct is one whose staff briefing room posts many photos of missing persons, young people—especially girls—who have disappeared and whose parents write, telephone, and come in from all over the country to find their sons and daughters. The precincts in the garment district, the Wall Street area, and the diamond market must be geared to deal with their unique problems just as the precinct house in the neighborhood of Times Square must deal with theater traffic, out-of-town visitors, and pickpockets.

The precinct houses located in German Yorkville or Irish Chelsea or in Mulberry Street or Second Avenue, with concentrations of the Italian and Jewish communities, have different problems from those located in Spanish Harlem or the Negro community in Bedford-Stuyvesant.

Just as the police have to have a strategy for diverse places so also they must be prepared to deal with diverse occasions. The visits of officials of foreign nations, the protection of the consulates of foreign countries in times of international tension, parades down the main avenue (especially when there are tensions over problems of war and peace and politics), "happenings" in the parks, fiestas—these place special responsibilities on particular precincts and specialized divisions of the police force. They are all part of the police job.

In this age of the motorcar the police have acquired an additional area of responsibility. To the regular flow of traffic are added the special problems presented by the morning and evening rush hour, the weekend exodus and return, the influx of visitors to the city on holidays. The police must clear the way for emergencies, for the fire engine and the ambulance. Just as the policeman must be alert to parking violators, speeders, reckless drivers, so he must also be ready to help the aged and the handicapped and the children who are not able to cross the street safely.

The police carry a responsibility for the maintenance of order in the community. Differences of viewpoint and conflicts of interest make for a certain amount of controversy. The police protect the climate of community security within which men can be free to differ among themselves and to differ with the government itself.

Thus police are called to protect the right to strike and to picket and the rights of property in labor-management disputes. The police are called to a legislative hearing when tensions and unruly behavior threaten fair play or interfere with the democratic process. Civil-rights sit-ins and demonstrations, the marching and countermarching by extremists of right and left, the "hawks" and "doves" in conflict over the issues of war and peace—these, too, require police presence. During election campaigns and on Election Day, it is the police who add confidence and assure the peaceable use of the ballot. Although police are citizens and human beings with their own viewpoints and their own biases they are required to exercise impartiality between groups. Insofar as they are able to achieve an effective and impartial role, they make a critically important contribution to the climate of community security and establish confidence in the democratic process.

The police are critically needed when a riot breaks out. When men become frightened and angry and desperate, when mobs form and the fury of a human storm looses violence in the streets, the people depend on the police to contain the fury, to curb the violence, and to scale down the tensions and restore order. The role of the police when a riot breaks out is one requiring strength and strategy, a judicious use of many forces, physical and psychological. It is difficult and dangerous to try to put down the fires of unreason and to do so in the midst of civil disorder bordering on civil warfare. But the bigger job is before riots begin: to carry on the police work of law enforcement and equal protection for all members of the community in the midst of deprivation and distrust and hostility. For though the police do not cause poverty and racial ghettos, they are the symbols of oppression. They are the objects of hostile feeling and have to protect those who reject them.

In the way the police deal with the intergroup conflicts and prevent civil disorder they can be a source of power to prevent the police state. For when disorder and chaos disrupt men's lives, they cannot find security enough to live in freedom. It is then that they turn to a strong man and strict discipline and yield their freedom to a dictator and a totalitarian state.

If crime and law enforcement were the only responsibility of the police it would be more than a full-time job. But the job goes further. A substantial part of police time and energy goes to dealing with human problems which have little to do with crime or the criminal element. Interpersonal differences produce a constant flow of conflicts between individuals: quarrels between members of families, between neighbors, between strangers and friends. Quarrels that originate over trivial differences often build up to serious assaults, injury, and even homicide. Violence may result from a traffic argument between two car drivers or between neighbors over a dispute about their children. Police may be involved through a telephone call to the precinct by parties to the dispute or by third parties. Police may also come on the quarrel as they walk the beat or ride by in the patrol car. These interpersonal conflicts require that the police intervene and restrain people from hurting others. They may require the police to mediate and help people understand one another and make peace. Where disputes involve individuals under the influence of alcohol or narcotics they may be difficult and dangerous. Where they involve the behavior of emotionally disturbed or mentally ill people, they call for sensitivity, patience, and psychological insight.

Whether the policeman is directing traffic, walking his beat, or riding the patrol car, he must be ready for dozens of different kinds of emergencies: the call for help when there is a theft or holdup; an accident in the street or factory or home; a heart attack or an attempted suicide; a woman in labor requiring emergency assistance.

Most civilians move through the community without ever witnessing an actual crime, an accident, a heart attack, or an attempt at suicide. If the civilian chances to run into such occurrences, he usually remains a bystander or walks away or simply calls the police. The police do not walk away. Emergencies are part of their job and part of their life.

When emergencies occur during the weekdays, police often deal with complaints and troubles by referring them to appropriate departments and agencies: the schools, the Welfare, Health, and Hospital Departments, Department of Buildings, Fire Department, etc. Formal referrals require paper work, forms, records. Many of the troubles are dealt with directly by police accompanying people to the responsible officials of these agencies. An examination of the number and concentration of emergency calls for police reveals that the calls increase in the evenings. There is also an increase of calls throughout the weekends. In part this is because it is during the evenings and weekends that people depart from their established movements in their work and home life.

People generally accept the fact that they may or may

not be happy at their regular work. But they expect to be happy when they have free time after work and especially on weekends. They relax, go to movies or the park, make trips, attend parties, and meet other people in relations outside the ordinary pattern of their lives. It is then that "things happen." When Friday, Saturday, and Sunday arrive, the frustrations of their lives, the lack of money, the sexual frustration, the frictions in the family—these become occasions for irritations and resentments. People take their unhappiness out on each other, on those closest at hand. What was to have been a happy outing to the beach or a visit to relatives or a movie or party becomes a disappointing, quarrelsome experience in which words and blows fly.

Another reason for increased evening and weekend police calls is the fact that professional workers and agencies usually are closed. The social workers and lawyers are away and the social agencies are locked tight. On weekends it is not only the poor but the middle and upper classes who call the police for help.

And when everyone takes a holiday, whether it be Christmas or New Year's or Easter weekends, police work never ends. A time of popular pleasure may cause more police headaches. The policeman will have to handle the drunks and pick the injured off the roads. Fires and fights and the results of the holiday aftermath are evident in the calls for help and the tragic scenes in the stationhouses of the city.

The police must be sources of information and serve as lawyers, social workers, mediators, medical experts, and psychiatrists. They must use authority with effectiveness, restraint, and impartiality. No professional group is on such a round-the-clock demand on an emergency basis. No other group is expected to perform such a variety of services.

Curses and shrieks come from a third-floor apartment. Someone calls the police. A patrol car arrives. Two police officers run upstairs. A man and wife are quarreling. Each is angry and violent.

"Get him out of the house! I never want to see him again!" shrieks the wife.

Each of the police takes the role of a friend, one of the wife, the other of the husband. To the husband: "How about taking a walk around the block? Give her some time. Maybe she'll cool off. How about it?"

To the wife: "Look, lady, do you want to make a charge? Do you want to go to court? Look at the kids. You've got a nice home. Give yourself time. Think it over. Once you go to court, you can't turn back. Better wait till morning. Think it over."

When they leave, one officer says, "Who are we to get in the middle of a fight between a man and his wife? And who are we to tell a man to get out of his home and take a walk around the block?"

The other adds, "We're nothing better than lousy social workers."

Factors That Make the Police Job Difficult

Modern urban conditions present particular difficulties to the police. In rural areas, small towns, and in villages, everyone knows his neighbors. Relationships are often friendly and cooperative. People count on each other in time of fire or sickness or other emergencies. But in the big city, although people pass each other on the street, sit opposite each other in busses, and are jammed against one another as they seldom would be in a smaller community, they are strangers to one another. This is true even for those who live in the same blocks or the same houses.

But in contrast with the large city, in a small town the police and the community know each other. Officers of the law call individuals by their first names, know their families and occupations, their habits and their characters. In the city, the relationship is for the most part impersonal, though it is true that in every precinct some police know and are friendly with many of the people.

Another difficulty lies in the mobility of the people. In the city, people are always coming and going. Besides the influx from small towns and rural areas, there is a constant flow of people from the South, from Puerto Rico, and foreign countries. Young people come to the city for many reasons. The migratory workers turn to the city when the weather gets cold and farm jobs are not available. People change jobs, firms reorganize, fail, move. People are intent on bettering themselves. And people move their residence, too. Few families or individuals in the urban situation live in the same place for more than six years. Buildings are torn down, areas are bulldozed, neighborhoods are uprooted, and people are dislocated without regard for the effect on stable neighborly relations.

To this kind of urban mobility should be added the impact of modern transportation. The motorcar, bus, and airplane increase that mobility a thousandfold. If the police have a problem of identifying individuals in the dense population and the impersonal community, even more do they have a problem of locating and apprehending the lawbreaker or the witnesses who might have information or help with his identification.

The impersonal and mobility factors in the city are accentuated when a substantial part of the population consists of people who live alone. These individuals include young people who want to live away from their relatives; those drawn by the glamour of the big city, or in search of careers; the homeless and unemployed migratory workers; the old people, widows and widowers; the unmarried women. Frequently they are unknown even to their neighbors.

Further complicating the policeman's work is the presence of people with diverse religious, racial, and national backgrounds. This was always a problem, especially in port cities with the precinct house in the heart of a newly arrived immigrant group. For the police the problem of communication was complicated by having to work with people speaking foreign languages—German, Polish, Italian, Yiddish—people with customs and traditions from the old country.

Difficult as this may have been in the past, it was easier than the problem presented by the present ghettos. The old ghettos were temporary: as soon as they could, the second and third generation moved out into the main stream of American life. Today, the people in the Negro and Puerto Rican community are in a more difficult condition. The Negro suffers from prejudice based upon his former slave status and the deprivation due to generations of discrimination and segregation. Although the Puerto Ricans, like the Negroes, are American citizens, they present some of the same problems as the older immigrant groups: barriers of a Spanish language and the customs and traditions of a Spanish and Caribbean culture. They, too, suffer from discrimination and segregation. The way the police conduct themselves with such groups is of critical importance. On the one hand the precinct house has been looked upon as a center of protection, a refuge in time of danger, and a source of help in time of trouble. On the other hand, it has been looked upon as a quasi-military fortress, an unfriendly place to be avoided. It is not easy for a police officer to walk his beat or ride the patrol car to assure law enforcement and to achieve good community relations and mutual respect and support in these segregated areas of poverty and minority concentration with serious delinquency and crime problems. It is extremely difficult to have such behavior reported, to catch the lawbreaker, to get witnesses or help in such neighborhoods.

All these conditions of urban life are further complicated by certain attitudes and behaviors which are not confined to the poor or to the members of minority groups. The police are symbols of authority. They represent the law and government. Many people—from many backgrounds—experience hostility to authority.

In a law-abiding community the people must know and obey the laws. They must also support the police in restraining those who disobey the laws. If the public fails to back up the police, effective law enforcement becomes difficult if not impossible.

The individualism and violence of American frontier society undoubtedly contribute to today's lawlessness. Too many individuals in every community assume that they are exceptions, as if the laws were made for the general public, but not for *them*. This includes public officials, political leaders, special functionaries such as business executives, doctors and clergy, and those who think that their wealth or social status exempts them from ordinary responsibilities. These exemptions are demoralizing to the police. They add to the climate of law violation. "If he can park here, why can't I?"

The ambivalence of the public makes for confusion on a number of issues of police operation. It increases the difficulties of law enforcement. It undermines and contaminates that most essential element, a genuine respect for the laws. Thus most people want traffic to move smoothly and quickly. But these same people double park their cars and do so on a main avenue at rush hour when traffic is at its heaviest. People park in forbidden zones, by the fire hydrant, in front of a hospital or school, regardless of the law or the safety or convenience of others. Most people want enforcement of the law that regulates gambling, narcotics, liquor, and tobacco. But they also want to gamble and to take advantage of benefits from the purchase of illegal items. Most people want beautiful and clean streets and parks, but they litter as they walk and ride. From the luxury apartments as well as the tenements, people who wish their own homes to be clean think nothing of throwing their refuse into the street. Like the children in school who break the rules as soon as the teacher's back is turned, so grown-up citizens exempt themselves from the laws and thwart the responsible work of their own law-enforcement officers.

Apart from the corrupting power of crime syndicates and political machines, every community has some people who can "fix" things by getting to the political leader or the district attorney or the judge. The efficiency and morale of the police are constantly weakened when valid arrests result in dismissals or token sentences.

One of the civilian attitudes which is perplexing and demoralizing to the police is the widespread indifference to the problem of the sale and distribution of guns. Civilians want protection and security. But civilian resistance to legislative controls presents difficulties. In the United States, the sale of guns to anyone, without any statement of purpose, without references as to the character of the purchaser, and without license or registration for future identification, vastly increases the difficulty and danger of the policeman's job. Even after incidents of violence and murder, the public has failed to give support to movements for the control of the sale of weapons. The guns lobby spearheaded by the American Rifle Association, with the support of the gun-manufacturing corporations, has succeeded in blunting gun-control campaigns. The apathy of the public has been a barrier to regulation and control. Citizens want the right to buy and use a gun without having to register or answer questions. Thus, at the same time that they express the desire to be rid of crime, they sustain those conditions that make crime easy and profitable. Criminal action is encouraged by access to arms. It is the police who have to face the danger in apprehending the criminal. It is the police who often pay with their lives.

Crime and delinquency are socially rooted; their persistence and recent increase are due to many factors. Programs for crime prevention must include making possible more stable family life, better child rearing, more effective schools and education for good human relations and democratic values, decent housing and neighborhood surroundings, adequate employment opportunity, advancement according to merit, and a more equitable distribution of income and wealth. To be sure, even under the most perfect educational and social system there will always be those whose personal problems lead them to commit anti-social and criminal acts. But these measures would contribute to a community life in which a much higher percentage of the people would achieve success without having to resort to criminal activity.

The police understand some of the causal factors in criminal behavior—that the public by its own behavior and its own neglect is largely responsible for the production of conditions which breed criminal activity.

Another ambivalence exists in the contradictory and changing attitudes toward morality. Although most of the community was brought up to believe in a certain minimum modesty in dress, there is a tendency today to accept extreme exposure. Marijuana has been forbidden under the narcotics law. Now it may be legalized. Formerly it was part of the Police Department's law-enforcement responsibility to apprehend homosexuals. Now homosexual behavior is becoming increasingly accepted when expressive of the wills of two consenting adults.

An added difficulty from a police viewpoint involves the concept and practice of "civil disobedience." The practice of civil disobedience as a legitimate means of social protest seems to have turned the law upside down. Now the police are told not to arrest those guilty of trespassing or meeting or parading without permit but to protect the very disobedience which violates traditional legalities.

The principle of obedience to law must be balanced with the freedoms of the First Amendment. But whether civil disobedience is protected under the principle of religious freedom and freedom of conscience or whether recognized and dealt with pragmatically as an instrument and a method in the democratic struggles of this period, the police have an added responsibility. Their directives are not always clear. Where civil disobedience is carried out according to the principles of non-violence its protection may have the support of the courts and the community. Where it entails violence, the responsibility of the police may be clear, too. But where it is non-violent and its non-violent action provokes violence by others, the police have to face added problems of policy and should receive clear directives for action.

Finally, recent court decisions protecting the constitutional rights of the accused now impose stricter standards and restraints upon the police. Police practices of search and seizure are now under critical scrutiny. Confessions or evidence resulting from coercion or interrogation of the accused without being informed of his rights or without the presence of his attorney are not acceptable in the courts. These court decisions make it more difficult for the police and the prosecuting attorneys to assemble evidence upon which to obtain convictions.

To the police the technical constitutional requirements may appear to favor the accused even when there is certain guilt. They may appear to work against justice and the good of the community.

But the courts as expressions of the enlightened conscience of the community are concerned that no individual shall be deprived of life, liberty, or property without "due process of law." Americans hold that a fair trial for every man is essential in a just and democratic society. Americans hold that it is better to have a guilty man escape conviction than have an innocent man condemned.

The police and the district attorneys may not like it. But what else is the function of the law if it isn't to assure equal protection before trial as well as during trial? "Due process" may make the job of police and prosecutor more difficult. But both must develop the competence which will guarantee basic rights and at the same time develop a strategy which will convict the guilty and protect the innocent.

Theoretically, in a society of free men the people are responsible for their own behavior. It is the responsibility of the police to protect the freedom of every man and at the same time to use whatever restraints are necessary for the safety and welfare of the total community. All men share this responsibility in a true democracy. For the police it is not just a citizenship responsibility: it is a professional duty as well.

The Gap Between

Historically the police have almost always been a reactionary force defending the king and emperor, the nobility and the aristocracy, the institutions of property and repression. Historically they are identified with the upper classes and against the masses. Normally they would tend to defend the employer and the factory against the workers and the unions, the landlords against the tenants, and in Western culture the white people and their power and privilege against those who challenge these.

As the police represent authority, they become the focus for all the resentments which Negroes hold against a system of law and property and politics which denies them equality of opportunity and a fair share of the good things of American life.

Negroes may feel resentment and rage against the landlords and storekeepers who exploit them, against the school officials who offer their children inadequate schooling, against the welfare workers whose decisions can be vital to family survival. Regardless of the good or ill of police performance, the police are a scapegoat for all other ills, for the police represent the entire system of confinement in the ghetto, the denial of opportunity, the deprivation which means poverty, and the discrimination and segregation which make for inferior status and humiliation. To the people in the ghetto the police should represent justice. But the police are the instrument through which injustice is imposed and sustained. By their presence they are party to the imposition of the whole ghetto imprisonment. The police, by their presence alone, are a constant reminder of powerlessness.

Whether it be in the Negro ghettos or among other low-income groups who are segregated according to color or ethnic or national background, the hostility toward the police has its ill effects on the entire community. It is in part responsible for the distrust of the laws, the courts, and the government. It is in part responsible for the failure of the Negro community to cooperate on law enforcement and to aid the police even when they are acting to protect persons and property in the ghetto community. Hostility is a critical factor among the conditions and forces which bring about racial riots.

Present-day Negro attitudes are conditioned by the actions of the police in the South. Just as immigrants from Czarist and Stalinist Russia remember the secret police, and victims of Hitler's Germany remember the Gestapo, so many Negroes remember the arrogance, oppression, and brutal acts of the police of the Southern states as agents of white racism. Since the Civil War the police role has been to enforce segregation and inferiority of status on behalf of "white supremacy." And today in almost every Northern Negro community a third of the people are originally from the South or have relatives there.

What are the grievances in the South today? In part police brutality. But also the underlying fact of racial discrimination. When a Negro is beaten or robbed or killed the white perpetrator is almost never punished. It is a rare thing for a white man in the South to be caught, arrested, tried, and convicted for crimes against Negro persons or property. In any difference of opinion or fight it is the Negro who is blamed and punished. If the Negro complains or seeks justice, he is considered "uppity" or a "bad nigger." The result has been the intimidation of the Negro and a fatalism about police behavior. The Negro attitudes grow out of long and bitter experiences that the police do not protect the Negro and that the police are party to the racist violence of the white South.

The practices of Southern police in recent years, the failure to protect the Negro in many situations, and the actual clubbings, beatings, use of cattle prods, shootings, and the injuries and the killings are all a matter of public record. It is now generally known that many of the police are themselves members of the Ku Klux Klan or the White Citizens' Councils. Many are confirmed racists. Their excessive use of authority and force to violate constitutional rights and to commit crimes has gone unpunished. Indeed, it has been protected by the political system, the courts, the juries, and those Southerners whose prejudices and fears and vested interests in the status quo of segregation are threatened by the movement for racial equality.

In the Northern Negro communities two charges are

usually brought against the police: first, that in the racial ghetto the police neglect trouble and lawlessness against which they would take effective action in the white community; second, that when police take action against Negroes, whether in the racial ghetto or outside, they are guilty of brutality, an excessive use of authority and force, and a violation of basic constitutional rights.

In regard to the first charge there is ample evidence from past and present practice. A 1942 study by the City-Wide Citizens' Committee on Harlem in New York City revealed that the police tended to look the other way when there were quarrels and violations of persons and property, and neglected to enforce the law on gambling, prostitution, and other violations. There were fewer raids and fewer arrests in Harlem than in other parts of the city.

Recently in 1968 a President's Commission reports: [1]

> The strength of ghetto feelings about hostile police conduct may even be exceeded by the conviction that ghetto neighborhoods are not given adequate police protection.
>
> This belief is founded on two basic types of complaint. The first is that the police maintain a much less rigorous standard of law enforcement in the ghetto, tolerating there illegal activities like drug addiction, prostitution, and street violence that they would not tolerate elsewhere. The second is that police treat complaints and calls for help from Negro areas much less urgently than from white areas.

[1] "The Problem of Grievance Mechanisms," *Report of the National Commission on Civil Disorders,* A Bantam Book, New York, 1968, pp. 307–309.

> In a United States Commission on Civil Rights study, a review of police communications records in Cleveland disclosed that police took almost four times as long to respond to calls concerning a robbery from the Negro district as for the district where response was next slowest. The response time for some other crimes was at least as long.

The Commission Recommends:

> In allocating manpower to the ghetto, enforcement emphasis should be given to crimes that threaten life and property. Stress on social gambling or loitering, when more serious crimes are neglected, not only diverts manpower but fosters distrust and tension in the ghetto community.

Wherever such neglect has been the pattern of police behavior, the argument for passing by trouble or incipient lawlessness has been that the police cannot act until a law is actually broken. A second rationalization offered has been that the people in the Negro ghetto do not have the same moral standards or require the same legal enforcement as the white community.

> The unstated and sometimes stated acceptance of crime and violence as normal for a ghetto community is associated with a lowering of police vigilance and efficiency when the victims are also lower-status people. This is another example of the denial of a governmental service—the right of adequate protection—which is endured by the powerless ghetto.[2]

[2] *Dark Ghetto,* by Kenneth B. Clark. Harper & Row, New York, 1965, p. 86.

Negroes want protection and law and order as much as other people. The vast majority are law-abiding and hard-working people who are struggling to make a home and raise a family. Their persons and property are the first targets of the delinquent and criminal actions which the ghetto condition produces. It is their homes that are robbed, their children who are hurt, their daughters who are raped, and their shops and schools and streets which are terrorized by lawbreakers.

The Negro prejudice and hostility toward the police begin early in life. The Negro child hears the talk about police brutality in the South. He is conditioned to distrust the police. He is indoctrinated with a belief that the police discriminate against people with dark skin in their enforcement of the law. As he learns that white children can do things and go places and have things he cannot, he experiences the unfairness of life. If Negro and white children become involved in a quarrel in school or on the playground or in the street, he may learn that the police chase the Negro children away. If such a conflict occurs when he is a teenager, he may be arrested and the white children may be let go. Such an experience will confirm his belief that the police discriminate. His feelings of distrust and hostility will be greater if his father or brothers suffer from brutal or humiliating treatment.

In *Dark Ghetto* by Kenneth Clark we see the resentment at what appears as arbitrary and unnecessary police action:

> . . . the officer said, "All right, everybody get off the street or inside!" Now, it's very hot. We don't

> have air-conditioned apartments in most of these houses up here, so where are we going if we get off the streets? We can't go back in the house because we almost suffocate. So we sit down on the curb, or stand on the sidewalk, or on the steps, but he came out with his nightstick and wants to beat people on the head, and wanted to—he arrested one fellow. The other fellow said, "Well, I'll move, but you don't have to talk to me like a dog" [Man about thirty-five].

> The way they'll do a man is something awful. And right in front of his family, of his own kids [Statement of a black truck driver].

Police action and attitudes do the worst damage when law officers touch a Negro man's relationships to his womenfolk and his children. One of the worst things anyone can do is to treat a man in ways which lessen his sense of his own manhood in the presence of those closest to him. He must not be humiliated in front of his wife or the woman he loves or his children. He must not be devalued in the presence of his neighbors and the community. Any man will seek to avoid this if he can. But to be insulted and humiliated and devalued by police whose authority and weapons and community backing put them in superior positions is a destructive experience of the worst kind. It is the hard reality that the Negro male has been subjected to insult and humiliation again and again and again by the white police of the South and the North. One such expression of attitude and action cancels out all the work of police community relations programs and police public relations efforts.

For the child the injury leaves a wound to the psyche which is ineradicable. The security of a child depends in the first instance on his relation to his parents, his trust in his father as protector of the family, his father's adequacy as a male, and the image of what it means to be a man in the world of humans. When the police by their action impair this, the tie to the father, the confidence in the family as a source of security, and the trust in the community and the world are impaired. Anxiety, tension, inner conflict, confusion about values and personal self-image and purpose—all these may result.

The power of the police puts the Negro male at a tremendous disadvantage. He may be a strong man physically, but he can be stopped and questioned and searched and insulted and humiliated by a policeman smaller and weaker than he is. He may be an educated man stopped by a policeman who isn't his equal in intelligence, knowledge, and culture. He may be a man of achievement and renown and character in the world. But the man in uniform with authority always has the advantage: he can detain, question, arrest, and humiliate him. The law-abiding Negro citizen has no security that he will receive fair treatment. If he asserts his innocence or claims his right to be respected with due regard for his freedom and dignity and privacy he may be charged with resisting an officer, disorderly conduct, disturbing the peace, or assault against an officer. The policeman's word will be taken against his own. It is this insecurity and the belief that his rights are not respected and that he is powerless against police abuse that account for the intensity of anti-police hostility among the Negro people.

Among the police, prejudice makes for attitudes of contempt and derogatory language and excessive use of authority and force. And the more the police are insecure or threatened in their own safety or their work of law enforcement, the more they are likely to do the very things which are violent and lead to violence.

Many police fail to differentiate between the minority people who are law-abiding and those who live by crime. When they do this, they do injustice and violate basic human rights. They alienate the Negro and other groups from faith in the law and government and in the police themselves. It is no wonder that the police walk their beat in the ghettos knowing that they are distrusted and hated and walking in "enemy territory." That the policeman is "the Man," the "Mr. Charlie," the hated one, is not new. James Baldwin expressed this in his "Man Alone" in the book *Fifth Avenue, Uptown*: "There are few things under Heaven more unnerving than the silent, accumulating contempt and hatred of a people."

There have been times in history and places on this earth where the police may have seemed to be armed to protect the people, but in truth have actually been armed to protect themselves. There have been moments in the recent past when taunts, insults, and physical threat and attack have tried the patience and tested the restraint of police. In its extreme expression the gap is more than lack of communication or cooperation. It is an undeclared but very real war condition between the people and the police. In the slums and racial ghettos of the 1960s the police have to be armed and have to travel in numbers and maintain speedy communication and transportation to deal with eventualities.

The fears, distrust, and hostility against the police are not confined to the Negro. Puerto Ricans, American Indians, Mexican-Americans, and other groups share much the same attitude. The degree of intensity varies with circumstances. As the Negro population is the largest among the minorities, as Negroes are the most articulate and best organized, it is they whose condition and treatment and programs for action engage most attention at the present time.

Whenever there is conflict between individuals and groups it is fair to say that the fault may be owing to both sides. Whatever ills there may be in the people's attitudes and behavior, the police cannot escape responsibility for the present situation. Police attitudes and behavior have helped to cause the gap between the people and the police. In part the situation calls for self-examination on both sides. Both have prejudices, and each tends to stereotype the other. As the people are ambivalent and want protection from the police so they also do many things which make it difficult to give that protection. As the police want laws obeyed and want support in their efforts at law enforcement, so the police also do things which alienate the people from respect for law and cooperation with the police.

In every vocation and profession the many suffer because of the malpractices of the few. In every functional group there are those whose prejudices and personal problems get in the way of good work. In every school there are a few teachers who fail in effectiveness because they don't understand children or because they fear them or don't like them. In every welfare department there are some case workers whose prejudices or personal difficulties with the use of money or authority make it difficult for them to meet the needs of their relief clients and the families entrusted to them. In every police department there are some men who are miscast.

In part the gap is due to the police lack of knowledge and understanding of the people of the minority groups. They often do not know the history or backgrounds or problems of the people. They often do not know the feelings or the deep needs and decencies of people who have brown or yellow skins or who speak a foreign language. In this the police are not alone. Some studies show that 85 per cent of the American people hold some form of prejudice, religious, racial, or national, but the police probably include a higher than average per cent of the prejudiced. This is curious since most police come from backgrounds of poverty and from people who themselves suffered from prejudice and discrimination at an earlier period. But when they face citizens who are poor, live in racial ghettos characterized by a high crime rate, some tend to believe that delinquency and crime and antisocial behavior are all signs of inferiority and degeneracy and fixed racial inheritance.

A number of attitudes do not endear the police to

members of the minority groups. Among these is the widespread police opposition to the abolition of capital punishment. That the police generally oppose any outside investigations of police affairs does not make people more trustful of the police. And that some police in the South are members of the Klan and White Citizens' Councils, and are members of the Birch Society and Minute Men in the North, does not add to a feeling of confidence that the police represent the interests of all the people or the support for the basic rights of all Americans. These attitudes and affiliations do not contribute to the communication and cooperation which are needed to close the gap between the people and the police.

The gap exists not merely between the police and the people of the minority groups, Negro, Puerto Rican, Mexican, Filipino. White and middle-class civilians also tend to have critical and hostile attitudes. In part this may be because of the American resistance to authority and interference with personal freedom. In part, it is owing to interference with property interests. The more people are able to own and drive a car, the more there are who have had a personal experience with the police. Most Americans are aware of the danger of speeding and reckless driving; most are aware of the inconvenience and danger due to illegal parking; yet the individual makes an exception for himself. He resents the man in the blue uniform who may call him on his delinquency and then write out a summons with its inevitable inconvenience and drain on his pocketbook and the record which may someday be used against him. In New York, when the police began to clear the streets for traffic by towing away cars which were illegally parked, it was the white middle-class citizens who stood in the street and hooted and shouted at the police, "Haven't you cops anything better to do?" "Is this the way you spend our tax money?" "Why don't you catch the muggers and stop crime in the streets?"

One key to an understanding of the people and the police can be found in the use of the word "civilian." Usually the word "civilian" is used in contrast to the word "military." The word "military" marks off those who are in the armed services, those who wear uniforms and carry weapons and fight in wars. The military services are the force which is supposed to protect the people and the nation. The fact that the police and the people themselves use the word "civilian" reveals a confusion. Are the "civilians" the people who are to be protected or are they the enemy? The word should be "citizens"—the people are sovereign and create their government and delegate to their officials a force to help maintain law and order. But it is the confusion about this very problem which helps make the gap between the people and the police.

In part this may be due to the people's ambivalent attitude toward the police as friend and enemy. So blind is the stereotyping of the police that if a policeman leaves people alone, he is neglecting his duty. If he acts, and acts well, he is interfering and is guilty of abuse of authority and excessive use of force. In such anti-police prejudice, the police are damned if they don't and damned if they do.

Some police attitudes and actions are due to the

character of those who are drawn to serve in the police force. As indicated earlier, they are influenced by their experiences as policemen and what the job itself does to them.

Studies show that police tend to be suspicious and cynical toward people. If they are less so when they join the police force, their exposure to the worst behavior in society tends to make them more so.

Some studies indicate that those who are drawn to the work of police tend to be "authoritarian personalities." The authoritarian personality tends to be rigid and fixed and resistant to change. It tends to see people as good or bad and behavior as moral or immoral. There is little ability to tolerate disorder even though democracy in times of change has to live with a certain amount of disorder. There is little understanding of the need for flexibility in the face of social change.

As Prof. Jerome Skolnick puts it,

> The policeman's role contains two principal variables, danger and authority, which should be interpreted in light of a "constant" pressure to appear efficient. The element of danger seems to make the policeman especially attentive to signs indicating a potential for violence and lawbreaking. As a result, the policeman is generally a "suspicious" person. . . . Policemen are indeed specifically *trained* to be suspicious, to perceive events or changes in physical surroundings that indicate the occurrence or probability of disorder. . . .[3]

[3] Jerome H. Skolnick, *Justice without Trial: Law Enforcement in Democratic Society,* John Wiley and Sons, Inc., New York, 1966, p. 44.

Police tend to be conservative. They are likely to be intolerant of intellectuals and intellectualism. They are also intolerant of deviants, of those who do not conform, of those who are "way out" or who stand for the "new" and "different."

> . . . Beginning with the fact that deviance may be a sign of danger, the police tend to see all deviance as dangerous. Policemen's work thus tends to make policemen socially conservative in the most fundamental sense. This has all sorts of consequences. For one thing, it helps to explain the strong negative responses that the police tend to display toward such events as picketing, wearing beards and sandals, and other socially disassociative activities. For another, and perhaps more practically significant [reason], the police are inclined to classify as crime all behavior that they see as discrepant with "ordinary" behavior, regardless of whether such behavior is technically a violation of law.[4]

Much of the policeman's business is to deal with the disorderliness of human beings. He has to handle the people that don't fit the norms of society and who strike out against others or act in ways which destroy themselves. The alcoholic and the addict, the individual who hurts others or appropriates property which doesn't belong to him, the mentally disturbed—these are the material of the policeman's work. He deals and specializes in

[4] Jerome H. Skolnick, *Justice without Trial: Law Enforcement in Democratic Society,* John Wiley and Sons, Inc., New York, 1966, p. 47.

social pathology. He helps to keep the social sickness within the bounds of manageability.

The policeman's work puts him in an odd and ambivalent position. On the one hand, he is the lowly public servant who walks his beat swinging a club, and on the other hand he is the great equal and master of everyone without exception. He has the authority to command or make an arrest of the most wealthy or best educated or highest official of the land. He may have no money but he can stop the millionaire in his Cadillac. He may have no education but he can demand the identification of the most brilliant of the intellectuals and make him appear in court for violating the law. He can take into custody the man at the top and make him appear like the lowest at the bottom, for the policeman has the power to shame a man. He can bring him down from high places. He can expose him, and if his good name and reputation matter, he can destroy him. This is the secret weapon of the flatfoot, the lowly policeman. He is the leveler.

Police Performance: The Plus and the Minus

There are those who are *for* the police, those who believe the police are always right and can do no wrong. And there are those who are *against* the police and for whom the police are a bad lot who are guilty of every evil in the book. The truth is never simple for any vocation or profession. For the police least of all.

More than most people, the police are criticized when they do the right thing as well as the wrong thing. The dice are loaded against them. No one wants to be restrained by an outside authority, a man in blue with a shield and the power to issue summonses and arrest and use weapons. This is true in many nations and cultures. But it is especially true in America where every man assumes he is as good as any other and can do as he pleases.

Sometimes the difference between the right action and the wrong action isn't clear. When is a policeman doing a good job? The answers to this question vary according to the viewpoint, prejudices, and positions of those who answer. For people differ in expectations and standards and they differ concerning when, whether, and how a policeman should act.

The policeman on the beat may report "no trouble, all quiet." This may have a couple of interpretations: he may be the kind who doesn't see trouble, is insensitive and blind, fooled by external quiet. He may be the kind who sees but turns his head away, is lazy, or doesn't want to get involved. It may be that he is corrupted and party to many things which go on under the surface of what seems like a "quiet and peaceful beat this week." Or he may be a policeman who is competent in dealing with difficult tensions and troubles before they flare out into real trouble, so alert to what is happening underneath the surface in a neighborhood that he deals with it before it can break out into explosive trouble. He may be quite adequate in his quiet way and so there is nothing to report. So also a policeman may hand in a report of many actions which may or may not represent good performance: he may be conscientious and zealous making arrests and issuing summons. But he may also be so callous and dominating and seeking for violent action that he actually creates the situations which require such action. He may not only not prevent trouble but he may even be the cause of it.

But despite all this, the conditions and police problems of a particular precinct and policeman may depend in a good part on circumstances which have nothing to do with a particular patrolman. The time and place of criminal actions or local interpersonal or intergroup conflicts or civil-rights explosions may have very little to do with the local police force. They may be the result of nationwide influences and the revolutionary temper of the time.

Plus

When people do their jobs well it isn't news. A man lies on his back on the sidewalk. Is he drunk or has he had a heart attack or an injury owing to a fall? He may be a character off Skid Row or a family man with a home. The man lying on his back is a Negro. Will that change the policeman's attitude and action? This Negro lying on his back has ragged and soiled clothes. Will that affect the policeman's action? Will it affect the judgment of those who are passing and stop to observe? One of those who stops is a young Negro. He has been used to the idea that a white policeman will never give a Negro the respect and impartial treatment which he may give to a white. What kind of police action is indicated? If it is a daytime situation, people are passing and observing. If it is at night, the street may be deserted and the policeman is alone. The policeman tries to talk the man into getting on his feet. He may examine him, smell his breath for alcohol, or see if he is bleeding. Is the man sick or injured? Should he call for an ambulance? If the man is an alcoholic, he tries to get him to his feet and on his way. In his effort to do the latter the policeman is firm and even rough—depending upon what he thinks will be effective. The officer talks to the man without getting a response. He takes hold of the man's arm and lifts and jerks him to his feet. The man's legs sag. The policeman holds him up, puts his hat on his head, and walks him around until he can move on his own. The young Negro waits until the white policeman has walked the Negro around and let him go on his way. Then the young Negro departs, apparently satisfied that there was no "brutality."

The millions of actions by police to aid the sick and injured, to settle disputes, protect life and property, to rescue people from a thousand crazy predicaments including being perched on tops of buildings or high bridge towers, caught underneath cars and busses and trains, trapped on rafts that are drifting down rivers or out to sea—the bringing of babies into the world and giving mouth-to-mouth resuscitation to all sorts of people—these are just a few of the daily good deeds. But the arrests for murder, robbery, rape, assault, arson, and the recovery of the millions of dollars' worth of stolen property and such illegal material as narcotics, liquor, smuggled goods, etc.—are beyond calculation. But even this doesn't tell the whole story on the plus side. For there isn't a thing we have seen on a movie screen or TV screen or heard on radio or read in who-done-its which has not occurred every day somewhere in the United States. Heroism isn't just in storybooks. For example:

It's ten o'clock on a cold winter night. A lonely patrolman is pounding his beat. He notices that there is a car parked in front of a liquor store. The lights of the store are out but the door seems to be unlocked. At the moment when he tries it the man from the corner newsstand comes up and says, "Two men with guns went in there. I think the old man who owns it is still there. Maybe it's a stickup." The policeman says, "Go telephone the precinct and tell them I need help." With his gun in one hand and his flashlight in the other he kicks open the door and calls out, "It's the police. Let the old man go and come out with your hands over your head." At that point the old man apparently makes a run for it and the policeman grabs him and gets him out of range. By luck he flashes his light on one of the gunmen. "Drop your gun and put your hands up!" he calls. The man obeys. He disarms him and handcuffs him and backs him out of the liquor store just as another policeman arrives. He hands him over and goes back in. In about one minute he has the other gunman disarmed and handcuffed.

The police expose themselves to danger. They bring in the desperate killers and gangsters. They are injured, knifed, shot, and killed in the line of duty. Many perform beyond the commands and regulations of the Police Department and are cited for recognitions, commendations, and awards.

Most citizens are unaware of the Honor Board as it functions in New York City and in many other cities. The regulations provide that when a member of the uniformed force performs an act of bravery or highly intelligent police work it shall be reported promptly to the chief inspector.

When the Honor Board has had a full report, the five top deputy commissioners of the Police Department question the policeman and ask for details. They want to know how he managed to handle gun and flashlight and handcuff the prisoners. They want to know how he protected himself, too. When he leaves, the Honor Board discusses and evaluates his performance and decides on the recognition and award he should receive.

There are eight degrees of departmental recognition:

A. DEPARTMENT MEDAL OF HONOR

Awarded annually to the member of the force who *intelligently* and in the line *of duty outstandingly distinguishes* himself by performance of *an act of gallantry* and *intrepidity at imminent personal hazard* to *life* with the *knowledge of risk above and beyond the call of duty.*

B. POLICE COMBAT CROSS

Awarded for successful performance of an act of *extraordinary heroism* while engaged in *personal combat with an armed adversary* at *imminent personal hazard of life* in the intelligent performance of duty.

C. MEDAL FOR MERIT

Awarded for an outstanding act of *personal bravery intelligently* performed in the line of duty at *imminent personal hazard* of life under circumstances *evincing a disregard of personal* consequences.

D. HONORABLE MENTION

Awarded for an act of extraordinary bravery intelligently performed in the line of duty at imminent personal hazard of life.

E. EXCEPTIONAL MERIT

Awarded for an act of bravery intelligently performed involving personal risk of life.

F. COMMENDATION

Awarded for an act involving grave personal danger in the intelligent performance of duty or for a highly creditable *unusual police accomplishment.*

G. MERITORIOUS POLICE DUTY

Awarded for an act of *intelligent* and *valuable* police service demonstrating special faithfulness or perseverance.

H. EXCELLENT POLICE DUTY

Awarded for an intelligent act materially contributing to a *valuable police accomplishment* or for submission of a device or method, adopted by the department, to increase *efficiency* in the administrative or tactical procedure.

Minus

Mistakes are possible and unavoidable in almost every profession. The police make mistakes, too. Some of them are understandable, some are trivial, and some are extremely serious.

Two policemen race up the avenue in their patrol car. They stop in front of a house, dash up to the front door, and ring the doorbell. They are in a hurry to search the house for drugs and drug pushers. A sturdy little woman bars their entrance. "We are police officers," says one.

"How do I know who you are?" says the woman. "You can't come in."

The first policeman pulls out a paper, flashes it at her and starts past. The woman hasn't a chance to see the paper. Moreover she is Spanish-speaking and cannot read English. She tries to shut the door. One of the policemen grabs her wrist and twists it. In putting handcuffs on her the policemen bang her against the wall and the doorjamb and scratch and cause bleeding on her wrists. They dash up through the house back and front, top and bottom, and find nothing and nobody. One of the officers takes a paper out of his hat and finds that it is the right address but the wrong avenue. They take the cuffs off the woman, and dash away to make their raid. Later they return to apologize. The woman is in a state of shock. She requires hospitalization. The complaint charges unnecessary use of force, use of derogatory language, and illegal search.

A man walks unevenly along the street seeming to stagger. Approaching a police patrol car which stops for a light, he is unclear in speech and unsteady on his feet. He makes some sort of request. The police take him to the police station on the basis that he is drunk and disorderly and disturbing to others. Later the complaint is false arrest and derogatory treatment. He is a victim of cerebral palsy.

A schoolteacher, mother of a sick child, is in a hurry to get medicine for a serious attack of croup. She leaves the child alone and drives to the drugstore. On the way she is stopped by an officer. She says, "Officer, you can give me a summons or arrest me but do follow me, don't delay me. It could mean the life of my child. He is alone; he could choke to death!"

The officer says, "You bitches think you can get away with anything." Then he deliberately takes a long time to write out the summons.

A man lies on his back on the subway platform. He is bleeding from his nose and mouth. Heavy snoring sounds come from his throat. A dentist who has excellent medical background stops to see what is happening. A policewoman is standing by the fallen man. She is asking questions of those who have gathered and is trying to get a picture of what happened. Apparently the man was struck by the train as he was leaning out over the platform.

"You had better turn the man over on his side or stomach," says the dentist.

"Mind your own business!" snaps back the policewoman.

"He is bleeding and he will suffocate and die unless you turn him over," says the dentist.

"Don't be a wise guy. I know what I'm doing," says the policewoman. "I've sent for an ambulance."

The dentist says, "This man is drowning in his own blood. It's keeping him from getting air. Turn him on his side or his stomach. Otherwise, he'll be dead before the ambulance gets here."

The policewoman continues to ask questions and writes her report. "Move along if you know what's good for you!" she commands. The crowd breaks away.

A Negro speaks:

"I have to deliver a package. I pull the car up to the curb and I get out. The cop comes up to me. 'You can't park here,' he says.

" 'I won't be a minute,' I say. 'I'm just delivering this package.'

" 'I'm giving you a summons,' says the cop.

"So I take the summons and I say, 'Officer, haven't you forgotten something?'

"He looks at me and says, 'What do you mean?'

"I say, 'All these other cars, these limousines, they haven't got any tickets. Why pick on me?'

"He says, 'What are you, a wise guy?'

"I say, 'Yes, I'm a wise guy.'

"And you know what he did? He took back the summons. The way I figure it, he must have been getting a payoff from those other cars."

Memorandum on Crime

When crime increases in the community some people attribute the increase to the failure of the law and law-enforcement agencies to bring the lawbreakers to justice. It is a common practice to blame the police or the administration officers responsible for police practice for the breakdown of criminal law enforcement.

There are others who see the source of crime in some one aspect of human nature or in one particular group in the population. Science has made it quite clear that there is no one criminal type, that there is no one physical or mental trait which can account for crime. Nor is there one racial or national group which can be said to inherit a tendency toward lawlessness and crime. Social environmental factors play the crucial part in determining whether individuals obey the law and carry the responsibilities of a free society or whether they are demoralized and influenced to anti-social lawless behavior.

The question is whether the experiences of the individual lead him to find that he can meet his basic needs so that he can work out a constructive life in harmony with society or whether his basic needs are neglected and violated to the point where he becomes destructive of persons and property and works out a life of lawlessness.

Three elements play an important part in this determination: 1. The stability and strength of the family *or* the lack of a family as a socializing and educative force. 2. Contact with and influence of adults who establish constructive human relationships and support democratic values *or* who, by their behavior, demoralize the young so that they cannot establish good person-to-person relations or find a basis for faith in their neighbors and in the community. 3. Contact with other children and older youth who have interests, motivations, and experiences which are constructive and lawful *or* with young leaders, gangs, and institutions which exist by anti-social and predatory activities.

The waves of immigrant nationalities which settled in the United States during the nineteenth and early twentieth century had to grapple with the problems of poverty and discrimination. Many of them lived in ghettos when they first arrived. For every group there were difficulties for the young people, which, in many instances, increased the crime rate in the years when they were struggling with adjustment to American life. The crime statistics of Chicago, New York, and other large cities in the mid-nineteenth century and in the early years of the twentieth century reflected the crimes not of Negroes, Puerto Ricans, or Mexicans, but of the Irish, the Italians, the Poles, and the Jews. These groups constituted the bulk of the prison population. But once they had begun to learn the language and find their way in the community, they or their children were able to move into the main stream of American life. In their schooling, their employment and their social life the young could for the most part participate in a process of integration.

The problem today is intensified and enlarged by the coming together of a number of factors which make adjustment difficult. The Negro community of the South has been moving North in large numbers. Those who have been the victims of discrimination and segregation, of racism and poverty, make their answer to life in a number of ways.

There are those who submit to the system which is based on the assumption of Negro inferiority. They accept the denial of their own basic needs to be respected and to have normal outlets for their urges and drives. Where outlet for the requirements of the ego is denied the individual turns in upon himself, with destructive results. He accepts his plight passively and dies internally. Many try to find escape in alcohol and narcotics and mystical experiences, religious and otherwise.

In contrast, many try to face the obstacles as a challenge. Despite all the difficulties and temptations, they struggle to get an education, try to get the best jobs they can, establish a family and live as law-abiding citizens. The tougher the barriers the more the energy and talent and effort they bring to their determination to make a success of their lives. They are sometimes the first to enter a particular school or get a job in an all-white firm or move into an all-white neighborhood. They are trailblazers for those who are to come after them.

Then there are those who respond to the condition of

their people by organizing or joining a movement to bring about social reform and social change. They may go into teaching or social work or the ministry. They may go into politics. They may spend themselves to use the democratic process to fulfill the promise of freedom and equality for all men.

But many young people in the racial ghettos feel that they are in a trap or a cage. They see no means of getting out. School is meaningless, and they drop out. Employment turns out to mean "nigger jobs," the most menial work, cleaning latrines, pushing carts of garments through the streets, shoeshine work. They have to get money to live, money for food, clothing, and shelter, money for the pleasure of cars, sex, recreation, and conspicuous consumption. Their experience has taught them that the world is a jungle where life feeds on life. They see what people do to each other, the brutality, the dishonesty, the corruption, and the hypocrisy. They meet the test of survival in the only way that seems possible for them, the life of delinquency and crime.

And some practice an active kind of idleness. They become involved in trouble, in the atmosphere of spontaneous or planned group violence. Where grievances and tensions have accumulated and feelings have been exacerbated, they become violence-prone and ready for riot.

Because there is a high incidence of crime in the racial ghettos, many people, including the police, believe that all crime is committed by Negroes and that whites are the victims. But a report of June 1967 entitled, "Crimes,

Victims, and the Police," by Phillip H. Ennis, senior director of the National Opinion Research Center, contradicts this. His study of criminal victimization, made for the President's Crime Commission, indicates that only 12 per cent of the crimes against whites are committed by Negroes. This means that 88 per cent of the crimes against whites are committed by whites. On the other hand, 19 per cent of the crimes against Negroes are committed by whites and 81 per cent by Negroes.

America has a history of lawlessness. It has a history of failure to catch the lawbreaker. In 1908 Chief Justice William Howard Taft said the administration of criminal law in this country was a disgrace. In the 1920s the Chicago Crime Commission declared that "crime flourishes because criminals escape punishment." In the 1920s only 14 per cent of the robberies resulted in arrests. Through the years only a small percentage of the lawbreakers have been caught, sometimes it is as low as 4 or 5 per cent, sometimes as high as 20 per cent.

To many civilians the police seem not to be doing their job. One study shows that an amazing number of people do not call the police even when an incident involves a crime and an act in which they have been the victims. The study reveals that of those who do not report the incident or call the police, 55 per cent do not think the police can do anything about it, that the police will not catch the offender, and that the police will not want to be bothered.

The police have faced many difficulties: inadequate selection, training, changing administrations, corruption, and the political practice of local bosses, who in many cases have controlled local precincts. The impersonal relations of the city, the high mobility of people today make apprehension of lawbreakers more difficult. But also it should be noted that when the police apprehend a lawbreaker it is only the first step in law enforcement. It must be followed by the work of honest and able prosecuting attorneys, courts, and by remedial programs for dealing with those who have broken the law. A very small percentage of those who are arrested are convicted, and when they are it usually is for some other offense.

It is no wonder that crime becomes a lucrative calling. Organized crime, racketeers, the underworld have long seen to it that the dishonest policeman is rewarded, the honest policeman is the enemy. In this they have often had as their allies local businessmen and local political bosses with the power to affect police promotions, assignments, to see to it that certain rackets were not disturbed, to penalize those who are honest and hard working in the Police Department. "Protection money" has been available from gambling, raffles, liquor running, that were not to be interfered with and also from thieves, swindlers, abortionists, and other elements all too ready to corrupt the Police Department. The Senate investigation of 1894 of New York City, the Seabury Investigation in the late twenties revealed how criminal activity was protected. Law enforcement was used for personal profit and is often so used today.

Riots

Riots are different from ordinary street fights between individuals, and from "rumbles" and "wars" between gangs of different racial and nationality backgrounds. Riots involve anywhere from 50 to 10,000 people. Riots are characterized by mob violence against life and property and public authority. Riots are triggered by specific actions and rumors.

In the Harlem riot of 1935 a Negro boy stole a small item off the counter of a five-and-ten cent store on 125th Street. The store detective pulled him into the manager's office. The store was full of customers, mostly Negro women. They believed that the boy was beaten. A hearse passed down the street and the rumor had it that the boy was beaten to death. In the riot that followed six persons were killed, 30 were injured seriously, and 3,000 persons were involved in the smashing of store windows, looting, and clashes with police.

In Washington, D.C., in 1943, white taxi drivers circulated the news that a riot would start at a particular place that night. This is the sure way to bring crowds together and to increase tension and create the condition in which an episode can trigger a riot. A demonstration and parade had been scheduled concerning job discrimination. Fortunately, the head of the police force did not cancel the demonstration but participated personally. There was no trouble.

In the Detroit riot of 1943 the Negroes were moved to riot by the story that whites had drowned a Negro baby and the whites were set going by a number of rumors one of which was to the effect that a Negro had raped a white woman. Neither rumor had any basis in fact. In the Detroit riot 34 persons lost their lives, 319 were injured, and there were 1,500 arrests. The city lost 1 million manhours of work and 90 per cent of its retail sales. Two million dollars' worth of property was destroyed.

In the riot in Watts, Los Angeles, in 1965, the chief of police had no real knowledge or feedback of the tensions which were developing in the area. Some of the most important top police officials were away on vacation. The communication system between police cars and headquarters was inadequate. Those few police who were performing their duties in the midst of a tense area misjudged the atmosphere and the attitudes and emotional state of the people. There weren't enough Negro police to make contact and communicate and help bring calm and order and restraint in the community. And once the riot exploded in full force, the police were let loose on the Negro community without restraint—all in the name of riot control.

For a long period before the riot broke out the Los Angeles police had been helping to worsen the attitudes and emotional state of the Negro community of Watts.

Negroes who had never expected decency or fair play from the police of Mississippi had hoped for something better in California and especially in Los Angeles. But the police harassed and hounded them. Stopping cars driven by Negroes, searches, rough talk, over-ready guns, insults, humiliations—for months these were daily occurrences in an increasingly tense atmosphere of insensitivity to human feelings. The complaints totaled 979 for the year. And there were enough charges sustained to result in discipline of the police force: three police were dismissed; eight were required to retire; 13 resigned rather than face disciplinary action; 88 were suspended without pay; 70 were reprimanded; 49 received admonishments, and four received warnings. 152 others underwent some other sort of "relinquishment." And all this represented the judgment of the "Board of Rights" of the Police Department itself. And what they were dealing with was only a small part of the vast number of cases of harassment and humiliations and violations which occurred and which were never reported or dealt with. When the police swung into action to prevent or control or contain the riot, they were not only at a disadvantage: they were looked upon as a causal factor, and they were a target of Negro hatred and a symbol of the "police brutality" in part responsible for the ills of Watts.

The failure of the Los Angeles police in dealing with the Watts riot was a failure to control a force bigger and stronger than themselves, a force so profound and destructive and wildly irrational and violent that it is a question whether any police or national guard or federal military contingent could have stopped it without massacring masses of people.

In the summer of 1967 a large part of the population of the big cities in the United States was uneasy. Both whites and Negroes knew that a long, hot summer could mean a long, hot trouble. Yet even those who knew the most and understood the danger had no idea that there would be so many riots or that they would be so intense in violence and so effective in destruction.

If the people of the cities were somewhat apprehensive and aware of what might happen, this was not true of those who lived in the suburbs or the small towns that are part of the suburban and metropolitan regional complex. In Plainfield, New Jersey, for example, the white population had failed to respond to the appeals and warnings concerning discrimination in housing and education and employment and recreation.

Yet it was in this quiet, respectable, orderly, and well-organized community that the people woke up one day to find that a riot can happen in a small suburban community, just as in New York or Chicago or Boston. For the young Negroes who armed themselves and taunted and hurled bottles and bricks at the police were not strangers from outside: they were strangers from inside, from the homes and schools and streets and growing-up places which had supposedly been part of Plainfield. They were part and also not part of the visible Plainfield. They had grown up with a different experience and had come out with a different picture of the common life. For whereas the white majority liked its life, identified with the authorities, and had confidence in the future, the Negroes of Plainfield, especially the youth, did not like their life, were not identified with the authorities, and had no confidence in the future.

When they attacked the police they were not just out for some fun as a college crowd might be. They were not teasing. They were enraged and bursting with the impulse to hurt and destroy and kill—to give vent to outraged feelings of anger and hate. They shouted what would happen to an officer who made the mistake of getting caught alone and without a gun somewhere near their part of the town. They made a list of the "ten most wanted policemen," and one of them, Number Three, was a Negro. In the course of the battle with the police 40 young Negroes trapped a white policeman, stomped him, cut him with jagged bottles, pelted him with rocks, and slammed a steel cart into his face. He died within an hour.

The killing of this policeman shocked and enraged the police and the citizens of Plainfield. The crime seemed worse because of the cruelty and ruthlessness. Yet the meaning of the crime seems to have escaped even those most closely involved. For the important element was the intensity of bitter and wild rage which led them to a completely irrational and bloody action. Their act was impersonal: they had no particular feeling against this particular policeman. He was for them the symbol of all cops. He was "cop-ness." And all the millions of unfairnesses, humiliations, intimidations of the years made this particular man in uniform a target. Yet the politicians and the people whose indifference and whose prejudices had permitted the conditions and policies which caused the riots seemed to learn little or nothing. "It's Communists!" "It's outside agitators!" It was only when it became evident that the Negro youth were ready to burn down the white sections of town that people generally woke up to the seriousness of the situation. Guns had been taken from the arsenal. A mob held the police at bay. Then the state police and national guard were called. Even then it was clear that the Plainfield mayor and safety director and police chief had no communication with the Negro community. They couldn't even negotiate. The authorities had no credit of good works or good will to draw upon in the crisis. Outsiders had to make contact with the mayor and safety director and police chief to avert a blood bath. Only because outside experts in race relations made contact and held off the police and only because certain concessions were made was the full-scale riot avoided. Those who were successful in cooling the situation and preventing an open and uncontrolled spread of the violence made the following demands:

> *that* the mayor and safety director and police chief meet with leaders of the rebellion and that they come into the ghetto area unarmed
> *that* the whites who were driving cars through the ghetto area be kept out and that traffic be diverted
> *that* at least twelve of those who were arrested be released on bail and that lawyers be permitted to consult with those who were being held.

Civic forces arranged for relief for those whose homes and food sources had been destroyed. Food was brought in. Welfare arrangements were made according to need. And then, as a final gesture, the troops and police were withdrawn.

Even people of tolerance and good will toward minorities do not wish to appease violence. But if it is bad to appease those who burn down the community and are moved by hatred and extremism, so it is bad or even worse not to do what is right and decent, and what is long overdue, and what is preventive of riots and constructive for all.

The danger is that some of the dominant majority will hold to attitudes of punishment and retaliation, that they will want more police, more vigilantes, more repressive and discriminatory policies. Many will say, "Arm the police with the most modern weapons for containing, paralyzing, and subduing people. Use tear gas, the paralyzing gas, tanks, and the latest Army equipment coupled with a get-tough policy! The important thing is to make sure that those who rebel will think twice. And the important thing is to contain the riotous behavior in the ghetto and not to permit it to explode out into the white community." There are many who think it is possible to keep the two worlds separated. And as long as trouble is kept away from their door, they don't care what happens to the other people, black and poor people especially.

Riots may be triggered by police action or police failure to act. But police do not cause riots. A police mistake or an action badly timed or extreme or in disregard of the prevailing social condition, can cause a crowd to collect and set off a series of emotional and physical events which can result in mob violence. But most often a riot is a sign of insecurities and fears and hatreds between groups or between those who are victims and their oppressors.

Riots are most likely to occur when new groups inmigrate and when their effort to enter the housing market, the job market, and the schools becomes a threat to those who feel that the community is theirs. Thus the arrival of Negroes (or Puerto Ricans or Mexicans or Filipinos) in various cities has added tension in the areas of "invasion." Similarly, Southern whites with prejudices and members of racist organizations such as the Klu Klux Klan have helped create the climate for conflict and violence.

When such in-movement takes place in time of job scarcity and the Negroes are unemployed and idle, they suffer from deprivation and have to become public charges or turn to extra-legal means of getting necessities, or starve. If there is a housing shortage and if they are hemmed in and denied access to housing outside the ghetto, if discriminatory practices deprive them of basic rights, the young lose the motivation to learn or to work or to have any hope of bettering their personal situation or the condition which confronts their entire community and race. Out of these factors young people can say, "The only way to survive is through violence that will shake up the white people and the white power structure," or "There is no hope. We are going to die anyway. We might as well die standing for something. Let's fight. Let's get the weapons and wage war. At least we can have some dignity and manhood before we go." Finally there are those whose pessimism and cynicism are so great that even the young teenager can say, "There's nothing worth saving in this country. Let it burn."

Riots may be aimed at whites, but it is the Negroes in the ghetto who are hurt the most. It is their homes in the ghetto, their public agencies of health and hospitals and schools which are prevented from functioning. It is their fire department which is prevented from helping in the emergency. It is the shops and markets which supply them with food and goods and services which are burned. Most of all they know that violence begets violence and that although violence by Negroes may dramatize their condition it may also bring about the backlash which will set back the hope of progress. Nevertheless, many Negroes have tended to identify with the feelings of anger and the desire to break through the feeling of powerlessness in the face of white indifference.

In the Newark riot of 1967 it was charged that Newark's law-and-order forces rode through the streets with rifles—for "fun," placed pistols at the heads of Negro youth forcing them to use foul epithets about their people, pulling the trigger knowing the gun was empty. In Newark, the people charged official indifference and contempt for ghetto leaders. The Negro attack in the riot was directed against the precinct station. Why? Because the leaders of CORE and the Anti-Poverty Program were refused permission to assist people who were under arrest and who charged (whether true or not) that they had suffered beatings and indignities.

In August 1967, while over eight hundred mayors and business, labor, civic, and church leaders were meeting in what was called the Urban Coalition to work out a program for urban America and prevent future riots, 18 Negroes filed a suit asking that a federal receiver take over and operate the Newark police force. They claimed that the police had consistently discriminated against Negroes and they named as defendants in the suit the mayor, the safety director, and the police chief. The suit charged that the Newark police had been responsible for a systematic pattern of violence, humiliation, and intimidation intended to deny Negro citizens their constitutional rights. It was also charged that the Newark police, the state police, and the national guard had deliberately destroyed Negro-owned property and had used "massive" and unlawful deadly force against members of plaintiffs' class when said force was unnecessary during the preceding riots. The suit also petitioned the court to direct the Newark police to cease from engaging in acts of violence, humiliation, and intimidation and the use of obscene racial epithets, the compiling of dossiers on civil-rights groups, and the arresting of persons for exercising their rights under the Constitution.

Once a riot begins, the police must bear the brunt of trying to restrain and control the extent of death and destruction. Other forces must also be enlisted to achieve contact with the leaders of the riot, with those (if there are any) who still have the power with their people to bring about a communication or a cooling period or a presentation of demands which might be dealt with rationally and humanely. The police have to know that force alone and police strategy at its best cannot do the job without help from the civilian authorities and the civilian leaders and experts on community conflicts.

The report of the National Advisory Commission on Civil Disorders of March 1968 (page 18) states:

> The maintenance of civil order cannot be left to the police alone. The police need guidance, as well as support, from mayors and other public officials. It is the responsibility of public officials to determine proper police policies, support adequate police standards for personnel and performance, and participate in planning for the control of disorders.
>
> To maintain control of incidents which could lead to disorders, the Commission recommends that local officials:
>
> Assign seasoned, well-trained policemen and supervisory officers to patrol ghetto areas, and to respond to disturbances.
>
> Develop plans which will quickly muster maximum police manpower and highly qualified senior commanders at the outbreak of disorders.
>
> Provide special training in the prevention of disorders, and prepare police for riot control and for operation in units, with adequate command and control and field communications for proper discipline and effectiveness.
>
> Develop guidelines governing the use of control equipment and provide alternatives to the use of

lethal weapons. Federal support for research in this area is needed.

Establish an intelligence system to provide police and other public officials with reliable information that may help to prevent the outbreak of a disorder and to institute effective control measures in the event a riot erupts.

Develop continuing contacts with ghetto residents to make use of the forces for order which exist within the community.

Establish machinery for neutralizing rumors, and enabling Negro leaders and residents to obtain the facts. Create special rumor details to collect, evaluate, and dispel rumors that may lead to a civil disorder.

The Approach to Civilian Complaints

Civilian complaints against the police can be handled in a number of ways. They can be ignored or repressed entirely. There are countries where no one in his right mind would dare complain of personal mistreatment or criticize privately or publicly the conduct of the Police Department. No matter what the violations of citizen rights and freedoms or brutality or invasion of privacy or abuse of authority, the people are silent and at the mercy of the police. This is one aspect of what is meant by a "police state."

In many American towns and cities complaints and criticisms are handled entirely by the Police Department. The police chief or the officers to whom he delegates responsibility decide whether complaints are to be investigated and what should be done about them. Wrongs done to civilians may or may not be righted. What is done may be entirely the decision of the police chief. The people may be unaware of their right to demand an accountability and a policy and procedure providing for receiving and handling complaints. Where the press and the leaders of public opinion are completely identified with the local "establishment," or power structure, the complete autonomy of the police and their immunity from any criticism or pressure may be beyond the reach of anyone—including the elected officials.

The extent to which complaints are welcomed and investigated and reviewed competently and thoroughly and impartially varies with the democratic character of the community.

The people and the city administration and the chief of police may encourage communication from the people free from fear of reprisal. When this is the case, the police chief may appoint his best personnel to do the job.

Another way of dealing with this problem is to set up a review board consisting solely of civilians. This is the kind of arrangement which exists informally in some of the towns and small cities across the nation. One or a few civilians may be selected by the police chief or by the town council to hear complaints and report them to the police chief for action.

For the most part the community hears little about it unless there is a case of flagrant misconduct by police and the case is publicized by the press. Civilian review boards have been in operation in a few cities. Doubtless many complaints have been well investigated and reviewed. But the general impression is that these boards have never had enough staff to process and investigate all their cases, that they have lacked authority to make the investigation effective, and that the flow of complaints has been disappointingly low. In one city at least the complaints were discouraged by the threat of counter-suits by the police on the grounds of defamation of character and perjury. With the increased concern with crime and riots, these boards have tended to fade into the background of public consciousness.

The awareness that there was a serious gap between the people and the police was evident in a number of American cities. Even before the Civil Rights Movement achieved a high momentum in the march on Washington and the pressure for a Civil Rights Act, Washington, D.C., and Philadelphia had established Civilian Complaint Review Boards. The word "civilian" referred to the source of the complaints. In Washington the Review Board consisted of civilians.

In New York City the Review Board established in 1953 consisted of three police officials. The investigative process was carried out by police officials. Complaints were received at Police Headquarters and at the precincts. Some of the complaints were dealt with at the local level. Some of the complaints were investigated by police members who were colleagues of the officers complained against. The weaknesses of this arrangement became evident, and at a certain time the Civilian Complaint Review Board was given a headquarters of its own away from Police Headquarters, and the investigation and review machinery were centralized so that any close identity of investigative officers with those complained against would be obviated. A separate and independent investigative staff was selected and trained to carry on its work in a central office removed from local and personal influence.

In the 1960s there began to be a demand for an independent Review Board to deal with the many allegations of police brutality and the growing distrust and hostility between civilians and the police. This probably was stimulated by the press and television reports of police conduct in the South during the efforts of civil-rights groups to remedy discrimination and deprivation in the Southern states. In addition, the demand came from recognition that the police misconduct was not confined to the South alone.

By the year 1964 the gap between the police and the people had widened and deepened. To some degree this was because of race tensions. The fear, distrust, and hostility to the police were a social reality. Damage suits and criminal cases against the police and the increased publicity given to incidents between police and civilians affected public opinion.

In 1964 Mayor Robert Wagner asked Deputy Mayor Cavanagh to form a temporary civilian committee to evaluate decisions of the Civilian Complaint Board which consisted of police officers. In his minority report to the City Council's Special Subcommittee Report on the subject, Councilman Aldrich proposed that the temporary civilian review committee be permanently enacted into law. Proposals of Council President Paul Screvane, Councilman Paul O'Dwyer, Queens District Attorney Frank O'Connor, Representative John Lindsay, and the New York State Association of Trial Lawyers, and the New York Young Democratic Club—all called for incorporation of a civilian voice of some kind in the civilian complaint review operations.

A bill introduced into the City Council was the occasion for much public discussion and different kinds of plans for an independent civilian review of civilian complaints. Those who supported the bill pointed to the many allegations against the police as expressed in the press and including such misconduct as excessive use of force, illegal search and seizure, false arrest, false imprisonment, delay of arraignment, incommunicado detention, violations of the right to counsel, coerced confessions, lack of access or delayed access to medical care, violations of free speech, petition and assemblage, the entrapment and harassment of homosexuals, the harassment of vagrants and derelicts, abusive language, and discrimination because of race, religion, and ethnic background or sexual deviance.

By 1965 a number of cities had experienced race riots. In New York the shooting and killing of a fifteen-year-old Negro boy by Lieutenant Gilligan triggered a riot among youth and extreme violence on New York's upper East Side. The lieutenant claimed that he had shot in self-defense. When the turbulence and tension had died down high police officials reported that their investigation revealed no misconduct by the police officer. Because of the public distrust, a grand jury inquiry was held. The grand jury found no evidence that the officer had been guilty of the criminal use of force. Yet the question remained: Was there no other way for the police officer to deal with a fifteen-year-old boy? Many still believed that the boy was not a dangerous menace to the officer. Could not a trained police officer have dealt with him without killing him?

Because of these factors, individuals and agencies concerned about allegations of police misconduct began to demand an independent civilian complaint review board. By this they meant a review board not dependent upon, or operating within, the Police Department and one whose staff and Review Board members would be civilians outside the Police Department.

At that time, under the old arrangement, complaints were received and were investigated and reviewed by police. All the operations of the civilian complaint agency were under the complete authority of the Police Department. The support came from the Police Department budget. The personnel were all employees of the Police Department. And if the complainant came to the headquarters or were involved in a "line-up" or a hearing he might well be the only civilian present and be completely overwhelmed by the feeling of lack of support. Approximately 90 per cent to 92 per cent of the complaints were found to be "unsubstantiated."

The idea of a completely *independent* Civilian Complaint Review Board outside the Police Department and apart from the authority of the police commissioner presented serious difficulties. It was argued that it would interfere with the clearly defined responsibility and authority of the police commissioner. He must be in control of the disciplines of his department. As for a completely civilian agency with civilians doing the investigations and the review of complaints, it was argued that only those who knew the nature of police work, its problems and conditions and its regulations and standards, could carry on realistic investigations and make intelligent appraisals and sound judgments on police performance. Just as the performance of teachers, doctors, and lawyers could not be judged solely by lay people, so it was argued that a purely civilian review board and staff would be incompetent even if it tried to be fair.

Apart from the arguments against an independent civilian complaint review board with civilian members and civilian staff, it was realized that neither the police nor the politicians would favor such a solution. The effort to bring about such a board through the City Council was defeated. Meanwhile, there was increasing demand and pressure to modify the Civilian Complaint Review Board which was completely staffed by police personnel.

It was in this situation that a *mixed* review board consisting of police officers and civilians appeared to be a possible solution. The proposed review board with a total of four civilians and three police might balance the fact that the entire civilian complaint agency would still be within the Police Department. Since the review board's recommendations were to be advisory only, the police commissioner's authority was unimpaired. The fact that four of the top supervisory staff positions would be held by civilians while the rank and file of the investigative staff were members of the Police Department gave assurance that there would be a greater fairness and at the same time retained the investigative skills of the members of the Department.

It was hoped that this compromise would be acceptable and that it would work better than a purely police-operated or a purely civilian-operated civilian complaint review board. Indeed, it might combine the strengths and advantages of both. The very fact that police were involved might make it acceptable and a source of security to the police. The fact that civilians were involved might win the confidence of the civilian population, and give security to the very sectors of the population who were most distrustful and hostile.

The idea of a civilian complaint review board consisting of police officers and civilians with a civilian chairman and with civilians holding the top supervisory positions was an attempt to meet two opposing viewpoints. It was a modification of the completely police-dominated Civilian Complaint Review Board setup as it had operated in the Police Department of New York City since 1953.

The Civilian Complaint Review Board of New York City, 1966

In his campaign for the mayoralty, candidate John Lindsay took up the idea of a review board with civilian participation as one of his campaign issues. When he took office as Mayor in 1966 Lindsay was confronted with the opposition of Police Commissioner Vincent L. Broderick, who resisted a review board including civilian members. The Mayor appointed Howard R. Leary as Police Commissioner. Commissioner Leary had been an excellent Commissioner of the Police in Philadelphia where he had worked well with a review board consisting solely of civilians. The new Police Commissioner put forth General Order No. 14 on May 17, effective as of June 30, 1966:

> It is the responsibility of a police department to stimulate and maintain desired standards of conduct by its officers. This requires procedures for effective discipline, including the thorough investigation and impartial evaluation of allegations of police misconduct. It is essential that the entire community has confidence in the impartiality of

> the administrative machinery which supervises the exercise of police power.
>
> It is the policy of this department to encourage the public to bring forward legitimate grievances regarding police misconduct. Every step should be taken by members of this department to ensure that complaints by citizens are received courteously and expeditiously.
>
> This department also recognizes that police officers are often subject to intense pressures in the discharge of their duties. They must remain neutral under circumstances that are likely to generate tension, excitement, and emotion. In such situations, words, actions, and events frequently result in misunderstanding and confusion. It is to the advantage of police officers to have an impartial forum for the review of incidents and the underlying circumstances so that unjustified complaints can be identified, basic misunderstandings can be resolved, and the complicated pressures of police work can be carefully considered.

General Order No. 14 provided for a mixed Review Board of civilian and police members.

"The Civilian Complaint Review Board consists of seven members. Three members shall be appointed by the police commissioner from the membership of the Police Department. Four members shall be appointed by the Mayor from outside the city government. The Mayor shall designate the chairman from among the seven members." (See Appendix I: Biographical Data)

The three police members appointed by Police Commissioner Leary were:

Edward J. McCabe, Deputy Commissioner in charge of Division of Licenses and for twenty-five years a special agent in the Federal Bureau of Investigation.

Franklin A. Thomas, Deputy Commissioner in charge of the Legal Bureau of the Police Department and former Assistant United States Attorney.

Pearse P. Meagher, Deputy Inspector, a twenty-five-year veteran and member of the uniformed police force, and the first member of the uniformed police force to serve on the police review board in New York City.

All of the civilian appointees were recommended by an eleven-member panel appointed by the Mayor to screen and suggest candidates for the review board and chaired by former Attorney General Herbert Brownell, Jr. From among the civilians suggested, the Mayor appointed the following:

Manuel Diaz, Chief Consultant and acting Executive Director of the Puerto Rican Community Development Project.

Thomas R. Farrell, lawyer, former president of the Bronx chapter of the Catholic Interracial Council.

Dr. Walter I. Murray, professor of education at Brooklyn College.

Algernon D. Black (appointed chairman), a religious leader of the New York Society for Ethical Culture and a member of the Board of Directors of the American Civil Liberties Union.

The seven Review Board members included four members who had law degrees; one was a civilian, the other three were the police officers, including the deputy commissioner for legal matters for the Police Department. The seven members included two Negroes, one a civilian, and the other a deputy commissioner. One member was Puerto Rican.

The purpose of a civilian majority was to overcome distrust by the public and to build confidence that the complaints of civilians would receive more consideration than they had in the past. It was hoped that the very existence of the new board would be evidence that the city administration and the Police Department were concerned with the treatment of civilians by the police. It was hoped that the police would be more aware of the need to respect civilians and protect basic civil rights. It was hoped that out of civilian participation a better relationship would develop between the people and the police. This could mean a greater community support for law and law enforcement.

In addition to the mixed Review Board the General Order provided that four civilians should constitute the top administrative staff: the executive director, a deputy director, who would also act as the conciliation officer, and two hearings officers. Under the executive director, the inspector and deputy inspector would be responsible for supervising, processing, and investigating complaints. The investigative process would be carried out by approximately forty police captains, lieutenants, and other personnel specially trained for investigation of civilian complaints against the police. There would be five to ten detectives who would constitute a special group for extra checking and the more difficult and complex investigative problems. In addition there would be interpreters—Spanish, Chinese, Italian, etc.—and adequate secretarial and office personnel.

Before the first meeting to discuss cases and review complaints, one of the deputy commissioners met with civilian members to screen candidates for appointments to the top staff positions: the executive director, the hearing officers, and the conciliation officer.

The screening and recommendations resulted in the following appointments by the police commissioner:

Executive Director: Harold Baer, Jr., lawyer, former Chief of Special Prosecutions Unit in the United States Attorney's Office for the Southern District of New York. Prior to joining the Justice Department he had been assistant counsel to the New York State Commission on Governmental Operations of the City of New York. As executive director he was responsible and accountable for the internal operation and activities of the staff.

Assistant Director and *Conciliation Officer:* Bernard H. Jackson, lawyer, who had served for four years as a patrolman and for five years with the Legal Bureau of the Police Department. He also had served as an assistant United States attorney and was regional coordinator for the United States Office of Economic Opportunity.

Hearing Officer: Henry Weiner, lawyer, experienced in private practice and experienced in conducting hearings for various agencies, private and public.

Hearing Officer: Daniel P. Hollman, lawyer, formerly chief counsel for the Coordinating Commission on Discipline of the First Department, and a former U.S. attorney with substantial experience in conducting grand jury investigations for the Southern District of New York.

Inspector Arthur Savitt and Deputy Inspector Jerome Stolk, who had come up through the ranks in the police force and who had been in charge of investigations of complaints under the old Police Review Board, continued to give their experienced services.

To prepare the civilian members of the Review Board for orientation in the organization and operation of the Police Department, the police commissioner invited the entire Review Board to meet with him and the deputy commissioners and the top-ranking members of the Uniformed Force and of the Detective Division. Copies of rules and procedures of the Police Department were made available to the members for study. Additional education and orientation experiences included visits to the departmental disciplinary trials, talks with members of the staff of the commissioner's Confidential Investigative Unit and the Youth Investigations Bureau, attendance at an Honor Board hearing, Precinct Youth Council, Community Relations Meetings, and tours of precinct station houses.

The civilian members were accompanied on these orientation trips by the police members. This helped the men develop friendly relationships. The joint interviews to screen and evaluate candidates for staff positions gave Board members added opportunity to know about each other's attitudes and values and ways of thinking. This development of respect and understanding made it possible to work together effectively. It was furthered by other experiences. The members spent quite some time working out the ground rules and procedures of the Board before they actually reviewed the first case. By the time the first review session took place, the Review Board was a working team.

It was agreed that one of the deputy commissioners of police would act as secretary to the Review Board and would keep its minutes. It was agreed that no verbatim reports would be made of the discussions of the Review Board concerning its procedures, its relations to the Police Department and the commissioner, or of the review process. The minutes, once adopted and approved, became part of the official record of the Review Board.

The authority of the Review Board derived from General Order No. 14 of the Police Department. The members of the Board agreed that any differences over the meaning or interpretations of the Order should be settled by the deputy commissioner for the Legal Bureau, and that if there were any differences beyond his interpretation, it would be up to the police commissioner.

The General Order provided that the Review Board should have investigative and advisory powers, not judicial or disciplinary authority. It should be up to the police commissioner's discretion whether or not he would follow the Board's recommendations. The Board would be advisory to the commissioner and would in no way interfere with the commissioner's power and responsibility to maintain discipline and control of the Police Department.

It was agreed that the Review Board would function in

private. In accordance with the General Order its sessions and discussions and decisions would be confidential. It would brook no outside interference in performing its duties and it would frown upon any publicity for its proceedings. If the members were to function in their impartial judicial role, they could not engage in any public debate. Thus all offers of the radio and TV networks to record and broadcast the work of the Review Board were refused.

It was agreed that the Board adopt a statute of limitations of ninety days previous to July 1, 1966, the date from which the Board was held responsible for complaints under General Order No. 14. Older cases would present difficulties of investigation. For the complainant it would be hard to bring witnesses and evidence. For the police officer it would be hard to recollect the case in its details. And for the staff, it would be almost impossible to keep up with the heavy backlog of cases as well as the complaints which would come in after June 30, 1966.

However, the Review Board agreed that the ninety-day limitation might be set aside if the executive director and the Board found reason to make an exception. In this connection it was recognized that some complaints would be delayed by the inabilities of complainants to cooperate with the investigation because of injuries, sickness, or hospitalization.

Another source of delay was soon evident in some of the complaints. It had to do with complaints which involved the complainant or the respondent police officer in court cases. If the complainant had been arrested and charged with a crime, the district attorney or the lawyer of the defendant might ask that the investigation of the case by the Review Board staff be delayed until the court had made its decision.

If the complainant made criminal charges against the police officer, this might also result in requests for delay of the investigation until the court case was decided.

And finally, if the complainant sued the police officer or the Police Department or the city, the attorney for the police officer or the attorneys and officials of the city administration might ask that the Review Board cooperate by delaying the investigation until the case was decided in the courts.

Damage suits and criminal cases by citizens were likely to be brought only for physical injury or false arrest. In most such cases there were no complaints to the Review Board. Among the complaints to the Review Board only a few were complicated by involvement in court cases. Where they involved allegations of derogatory treatment, discourtesy, racial slurs, etc., the courts could not deal with them under the law. But where complaints did involve court cases, the result could delay the Review Board investigation for a long time.

An example of such a case: a complainant alleged that he was assaulted by a policeman and that as a result he sustained abrasions, bruises, and contusions on the left side of the head and that he required suturing and treatment at one of the city hospitals. Investigation disclosed that the complainant did receive the injuries described, and did have hospital care. The complaint charged brutality, excessive use of force, assault and battery. The damage suit against the police and the city charged assault and battery and asked compensation for loss of earnings. The comptroller of the city and the attorney for the complainant both requested that the Review Board should not process the case until the civil action had been concluded in the courts.

It was agreed that when a case was before a criminal court it would not be the subject of investigation if the attorney for the complainant or the district attorney requested that the Civilian Complaint Review Board hold off until the case was settled. It was agreed that in civil damage suits against the police and the city, investigation would wait on the notice from the city comptroller or the city corporation counsel. The Review Board investigation could proceed if it so decided. But in most cases it would cooperate with the attorneys in a case, the district attorney, the city comptroller, or city corporation counsel when they requested a delay.

It was important for the Review Board and the investigating staff to be clear on the areas of jurisdiction assigned to the review agency. Some complaints could be recognized immediately to be outside its jurisdiction. Some would seem to be appropriate to the Review Board but investigation might reveal that they belonged elsewhere. In both kinds of cases the complaints would be referred to appropriate agencies. General Order No. 14, which established the Civilian Complaint Review Board, clarified the areas of jurisdiction:

> The Board shall have the power to investigate and to review allegations of misconduct by members of the Department involving:

a. Unnecessary or excessive use of force.
b. Abuse of authority (includes unreasonable action taken in an official capacity which deprives individuals of rights guaranteed by law).
c. Discourtesy, or abusive or insulting language.
d. Language, conduct, or behavior which is derogatory to a person's race, religion, creed, or national origin.

Complaints of any nature could be made at any time at the office of the Civilian Complaint Review Board, at any office or precinct house of the Police Department, or through the office of the Mayor or the police commissioner. Complaints could be filed by any interested person or group. Complaints could come from organizations such as the Legal Aid Society, the New York City Commission on Human Rights, the American Civil Liberties Union, National Association for the Advancement of Colored People, the Urban League, CORE, and other agencies and local groups.

Complaints could be accepted in writing, in person, or by telephone whether or not the complainant offered his name.

It was agreed that the report on investigation of complaints should indicate the color or ethnic or national background of both the complainant and the policeman accused. Without this information it would be impossible to know what part racial and other differences had played in the case.

On the back of each complaint a notation was made by

the individual receiving the complaint indicating the condition of the complainant, whether sober or under the influence of alcohol or drugs, whether calm and coherent or disoriented and excited.

When complaints were made they were entered upon a special form, "U 245," and were recorded in a ledger so that no case could be lost or forgotten. Complaints were acknowledged in writing. A captain was assigned to investigate the case. His job was to identify the officer against whom the complaint was lodged. If the name or shield number were not available he might be able to identify the officer through the local precinct and the assignments of particular officers at the time in question. If he could not locate the officer to acquaint him with the allegations and question him, then it might be necessary to have a line-up to give the complainant an opportunity to identify the officer.

> 21/9.1 In attempting to identify the member or members, a line-up of at least six members of the force shall be used if possible. They shall be in uniform or civilian clothes according to the nature of the complaint. When in uniform, they shall not wear shields, cap devices or other identifying insignia. Such line-up shall be conducted without unnecessary delay.
>
> 21/9.2 During such a line-up, a trustee or other representative of a line organization and the attorneys or other representatives of the complainant and the member or members complained of may be present. Under no circumstances, however, shall any such representatives be permitted to par-

ticipate in any manner other than as observers.
(G.O. 14, s. 1966)

The Board agreed that the police officer should be informed of the complaint and allegations against him, that he had the right to counsel, and that an attorney would be provided by himself, by the Patrolmen's Benevolent Association, the Police Department, or by the Review Board.

The Board agreed that the police officer is in an employer-employee relationship and that the officer is not under arrest nor in custody, and that he should be available and ready to answer the allegations. In order to assure the police protection of their rights, the Review Board agreed that the chairman, the deputy commissioner for the Legal Bureau, and the executive director, should meet with the attorney representing the Patrolmen's Benevolent Association to work out the procedures that would assure fair treatment.

When the complaint supervisor was satisfied that the investigation had gone as far as it could, it would be checked by the executive director. If he was satisfied that it was ready for review, the report would be duplicated so that each member of the Review Board could study the case. This required seven individual reviews before the Review Board came together. Each member was to do his homework by marking the case: "R" for referral, "U" for unsubstantiated, "C" for conciliation, "H" for a further hearing, and "Ch" for *charges*.

These seven individual "reviews" were then pooled in the meetings of the Review Board. It was agreed that if the individual conclusions differed by as much as one vote, there would be a discussion of the differences and the issues involved. It was also agreed that even where there was unanimity, the complaint case would be discussed in the following instances:

If the case was serious enough to warrant a "hearing" or if the Review Board recommended "charges" to the commissioner.

If there was any unique characteristic or question or misunderstanding which merited exploration.

Where "charges" were made, they were forwarded immediately to the police commissioner for his approval. Unless they were returned to the Review Board for further consideration, they were, if approved by the police commissioner, sent on to the deputy commissioner for trial.

When "charges" were recommended, the parties were notified by the trial room. With respect to recommendations other than "charges," letters were prepared over the signature of the executive director and sent along to Headquarters for approval by the police commissioner. Such letters to the complainant and to the member of the force involved were forwarded by certified mail. Form letters were developed to cover the various classes of complaints but were often personalized to cover specific situations.

For accusations and charges of police misconduct which are outside the areas of jurisdiction of the Civilian Complaint Review Board, the Police Department holds "disciplinary trials." These cover violations of police disciplines and dishonesties in the performance of duty, failure to carry out assignments, graft and corruption, false reports to superior officers, etc.

In one case a police officer turned in a report which would assure him a reward, commendation, and promotion. He claimed to have stopped a murderous fight, to have fired shots in the air, disarmed a dangerous armed assailant, and arrested him. It turned out that he had fired two shots into the river to corroborate his report that he had had to use his gun in action. In another case the charge held that the gasoline tank in the precinct station house parking lot had been used for the private car of a policeman. It was charged that the attendant was paid a small fee for making available city-owned gasoline.

The disciplinary trials conducted by one of the deputy commissioners are adversary proceedings with charges against the police officer and the presentation of evidence by the Department attorneys. The trials are public. The "due process" protections are observed. But the trials are tough and the police do not relish having to face charges at Headquarters.

Instructions

The Review Board had been in operation only a few weeks when it became evident that some kinds of complaint were not adequately provided for by the General Order No. 14. For example, there were cases in which police misconduct was proved but was not serious enough to warrant sending a recommendation of "charges" to the police commissioner. Review Board and staff members recommended an intermediate type of action which would satisfy the complainant and improve the police officer's understanding of his job and better his performance. It was agreed that "instructions" might be given to the accused officer by someone on the uniformed police force, the complaint supervisor or the line officer in the local supervisory office. Some cases which fell under this category were as follows:

A police officer stopped a motorist for a routine check and found that his operator's license had expired. The officer was accompanied by a probationary patrolman. As the officer started to write the summons, the complainant asked to be given a "break" and simultaneously started to take down the officer's shield number. The probationary patrolman thereupon interfered and addressed the complainant in a profane and vulgar manner. The older officer told the probationary man to go away, and he then completed his police business with the complainant. Instructions were given to the probationary patrolman as to the manner in which he was expected to perform his role as a police officer.

This complaint arose out of a minor accident between complainant's auto and a bus, involving only property damage: The patrolman witnessing the collision thought that the complainant was making too much of it and sought to dissuade him from exchanging licenses with the bus driver. Ten minutes after the incident occurred, the officer issued a summons to the complainant for failing to signal, stating to him, "How stupid can you get?" Instructions were given the officer as to proper police functions in traffic situations and effectiveness of good public relations.

If cases were found to be "unsubstantiated" or if they were "conciliated," no notation of the complaint was sent to Police Headquarters or the precinct station house. Nor was there any notation placed in the policeman's career folder. Only in the cases referred for "charges" were the reports sent to the police commissioner and the case noted in the policeman's career folder.

In cases marked "unsubstantiated" or "conciliated" the police officer received a letter in which it was expressly stated that there would be no notation on the officer's record and no notation in his career folder.

On Civilian Complaints

The metropolitan area includes 8 million residents, and attracts commuters, shoppers, theater-goers, and visitors. It is served by approximately twenty-eight thousand police covering a twenty-four-hour-day and seven-day week. The number of contacts between the people and the police is enormous. No one can know or estimate the number of incidents involving misunderstandings, mistakes, and misconduct which might be grounds for complaints.

For a number of years the old Complaint Review Board averaged only about two hundred complaints a year; in 1964 there were 231. After the new and mixed civilian-police review board was appointed in July 1966, the complaints began to come in at the rate of 90 to 110 per month, totaling 440 complaints during the four months of its existence. (See Appendix II: Volume of Complaints). Why this increase? Part of it was owing to the fact that the new, mixed Review Board was the subject of much discussion and controversy. The election and referendum campaign from July to November brought it widespread publicity. The fact that now civilians were members of the top investigating staff and of the Review

Board itself gave people confidence that their complaints might receive careful and impartial investigation and review.

Another factor was to be found in the conditions which prevailed in the summer of 1966. The hot weather and the water shortage made for more than the usual discomfort and irritations. More than ever, people, especially in the racial ghettos, tried to find relief in the streets. The collision of people with different needs, interests, and viewpoints each with their respective fears and prejudices, made for interpersonal and intergroup incidents which in many cases involved police action.

The total for the entire year of 1966 came to about one thousand complaints. The number per month fell off in November and December, owing in part to the defeat of the Civilian Complaint Review Board at the polls, and in part to the winter weather which kept people off the streets. The number of complaints mounted again to one hundred a month in January 1967, and continued with 1,300 complaints for 1967 even though there were no longer civilians on the Board. This increase was probably because of the widespread publicity, which for the first time gave knowledge and information to the people that there was an agency and a place where complaints could be received.

Despite this continuing increase, the total or over-all number of complaints is low relative to the enormous size of New York City. Some will argue that the low number is owing to the fact that most people are law-abiding and have very few encounters with the police, or that most of the police carry out their duties very well.

But possibly there are far more civilian grievances than complaints to the Review Board. The number of complaints may be in the same relation to the number of provocations as the visible tip of an iceberg is to the large ice mass hidden under the surface of the sea. No one would claim that the small number of complaints brought to the Human Rights Commissions under the Fair Employment and Fair Housing Laws is an adequate index of the extent of discrimination and segregation actually practiced. There may be, and probably are, many grievances which never take the form of complaints.

A substantial number of complaints are outside the jurisdiction of the Civilian Complaint Review Board. Many of these are complaints by citizens who have been victims of graft, corruption, and extortion. Some come from citizens who have observed or have evidence of various forms of "payoffs" and "takes" and "protection money" which passes from petty racketeers to police in order to protect narcotics, prostitution, and "numbers." Some involve the relationships between organized crime syndicates and the police. Such complaints go to the Mayor, the police commissioner, and the city director of investigations. It is estimated that an average of eighty complaints a month come to the office of the director of investigations.

Quite a number of serious complaints against the police take the form of court cases: civil suits against the police and the city; criminal charges for injuries resulting from assault and battery.

One factor making for fewer complaints is not generally known. Not infrequently in the courts, charges against citizens are dropped on condition that the defendant agree not to sue the city and the police and not to make a civilian complaint against the police. Why does the district attorney's office become party to such agreements? Why do judges permit such "deals"? The practice is frustrating and destructive of the free and fearless flow of complaints. The complaints are stifled at birth.

Some complaints—and it is difficult to know with accuracy exactly how many there are—may be handled at the precinct station. But the Police Department General Order No. 14 requires that such complaints be passed on to the Review Board headquarters. Subsequent complaints to the Review Board revealed that some complaints made in the precincts had not been forwarded. Failure to report and pass on all complaints to the Civilian Complaint Review Board headquarters could result in serious disciplinary action.

No doubt some of the complaints are based upon ignorance and misunderstandings. Some may be due to hostility against the police and constitute a form of harassment. Some are because of the tendency of minority groups to assume that any form of police action against them is motivated by racial prejudice and discrimination—this even when there is no valid basis for the assumption.

Many incidents might occasion complaints which are never made. There are many reasons for this. Most people accept mistakes and mistreatment by a salesperson or a bus driver or train conductor without taking the trouble to do anything about it besides grumble. If the complaint is against a government department, people assume that it will get lost or thrown out, or be evasively or defensively dealt with by the "bureaucracy." Further, many people believe that the police are an extremely tight "closed corporation," that they will cover up for each other; that they do not testify against each other if they can help it. The policeman who would expose a fellow officer would risk a great deal in trust and comradeship in the future, and possibly endanger his career, his future promotion. This fraternal and mutually protective spirit is similar to the situation in the military forces, especially intense where the alleged offender is an officer.

Many people are timid, especially when it comes to criticizing the police. They do not want to do anything which might result in an investigation and the possibility of having to come to a hearing to confront the person they accuse of mistreating them. Some have a record and have reason to hide some past action, afraid it may be used against them. If a man is actually arrested, he may be reluctant to file a civilian complaint for fear that it will cause the police to make an extra effort to have him convicted with the hope of weakening the case for his complaint. The lawyer for an individual facing trial often advises him that filing his complaint will jeopardize his chances of getting off on the charges against him. Another may have no arrest in his record, but may have done something which he wishes to hide: he may have entered the country illegally, or been involved in payoffs, and so on.

The complainant may lack witnesses or evidence to support his grievance. He may fear countercharges, that he is mistaken in his facts, that he has falsified his account, that he was drunk or emotionally disturbed, that he is not without blame for the incident. There is often a fear that the complainant might be prosecuted for perjury in the event that his allegations cannot be proved. With this goes the fear of a counter defamation suit by the police. Although such suits have been known in Washington, D.C., the New York City administration and the courts have attempted to give security against such actions.

Then there is the fear of possible retaliation—the owner of a house, or a business, the possessor of a license may, whether warranted or not, fear that if he makes a complaint he will be harassed with "violations"; the person on welfare or living in a public housing project may dread the loss of some benefit.

In addition, the poor man may be ignorant of the law and his rights, unaware of procedures and protections or unable to afford a lawyer. He may have a blind fear of the police and the precinct house. He may also be advised by his more timid relatives or neighbors that more harm is likely to result if he tries to do anything. Such fears are particularly prevalent among minority groups, and may well account for the fact that the number of complaints from such groups is not larger.

Out of one hundred civilian complaint cases, over half arose from white civilians against white police. In most of the cases that came before the Review Board there was no racial or religious or nationality issue. However, as expected, it was in the cases where the policeman was white, or identified with a particular religion or nationality, and the civilian was of another background, that the complaint charged prejudice and discriminatory treatment.

Of the 440 complaints which were received by the Civilian Complaint Review Board from July 1 through November 8, 1966, 220 came from white civilians and 150 from Negro civilians. (See Appendix III: Ethnic Origin of Complainants). If the 60 complaints received from Puerto Ricans and other minorities were added to the complaints from Negroes, the total would constitute one half of all complaints received during the four months. The percentage of complaints from Negroes, Puerto Ricans, and other minority groups in relation to those from white complainants should be evaluated. It is likely that many incidents and grievances were never brought to the attention of the Board, since it is the poor, the foreign-language groups, and the Negroes who were most likely to be unaware of the existence of the Review Board or to have no faith that their complaints would be considered or dealt with justly.

Although complete accurate statistics on the civilian complaints which came in during the four months of the Review Board's operation are not possible, nevertheless, some facts are available.

Most complaints were made in person and by telephone, some by letters.

Out of 440 complaints, over 200 were made in person and 150 by telephone.

Most of the incidents in which mistreatment was alleged occurred between 4 P.M. and midnight and most of them on Saturdays.

Most of the incidents and "mistreatments" occurred in the streets. Two other places mentioned most frequently were in residences and in station houses.

Most complaints came in through the C.C.R.B. headquarters, the next largest number through field units. A few came through the commissioner's office and Mayor's office and a very few through news stories in the mass media.

Male complainants outnumbered female complainants two to one.

Many of the complaints which flowed into the Review Board had nothing to do with crime. Often they originated in interpersonal arguments and quarrels between members of families, neighbors, in the frictions and hostilities between people in cars and bars, and in the streets.

"Cars and bars" accounted for a large proportion of the incidents: the traffic violator, the illegal parker, the impatient or abused taxi driver are likely to feel and resent the authority of the law. Some have trouble accepting a summons even when they have it coming to them. Those involved in a collision usually tend to blame the other party and expect the police to support them. Many incidents occurring in or outside of bars were inevitably aggravated when the complainant had been drinking.

Among the allegations, "unnecessary force" was the most frequent, constituting approximately half of the total. (See Appendix IV: Nature of Allegations). Next came the allegations of "discourtesy" and "derogatory treatment." "Abuse of authority" came third and "racial slurs" and insulting language came last.

The cases arising out of civil-rights situations, out of demonstrations, sit-ins, parades, or even after interracial dances or meetings on the race question, while comparatively few in number, presented the greatest difficulty, the greatest challenge.

Among the "interested parties" who complained or were party to the consideration of a case during investigation, or hearing, were the following: Attorneys, CORE, the newspaper *El Diario,* the New York Civil Liberties Union, the N.A.A.C.P. Legal Defense and Education Fund, the Student Non-Violent Coordinating Committee, the Brownsville Community Council, the New York City Commissioner on Human Rights, and the district attorney.

In the mind of the civilian who alleges mistreatment there is always the assumption that the reason for it was the prejudiced attitude of the police. Certainly the hostility between police and citizen is intensified when the civilian represents more than one of the groups against which there is prejudice—or even a legitimate distrust. Thus the policeman will be quick to stop the teenager driving a car. Triple prejudice is likely to be aroused when he confronts a teenage Negro, who is a militant civil-rights worker sporting a civil-rights bumper sticker on his car. A young Negro merely carrying a package may arouse a policeman's suspicions because of the possibility of theft or the possession of narcotics, and from this triple association the officer may react with particular zeal and aggressiveness. And when the policeman reacts out of insecurity or fear in a poverty or ghetto area, he may see evils which are not there, and by his action generate the very militant reaction which is most difficult for him to handle.

While the number of complaints which flow into a Review Board may be a partial indicator of the state of the relationship of the police to the civilian population, it is not necessarily the most meaningful measure. The kinds of complaints, their origin and motivations, may be even more important as a key to police and community relationships.

The Classification of Civilian Complaints

When complaints had been investigated and the findings and recommendations were ready for reference to the Review Board, each member studied each case, and the Review Board members then met together for review sessions where cases were discussed and judgments pooled. In the weekly review sessions the complaints were disposed of under the classifications of "referred," "unsubstantiated," to be "conciliated," or for further investigation through "hearings," or "charges." Some cases were sent back to the staff for further investigation when the Review Board was dissatisfied with the investigation report and felt that more could be done to get the facts.

Referred

Those civilian complaints which were investigated and found to concern matters outside the four jurisdictions of the Civilian Complaint Review Board were marked "R" and referred to the appropriate agencies.

Cases involving members of the New York City Police Department outside of the four areas of jurisdiction of General Order No. 14 were referred to the chief inspector. Such cases might involve drunkenness, failure to report on duty, graft and corruption, etc. Some cases involving personal problems were referred to a police officer's immediate superior, the precinct captain. Some involved the kind of counseling which the officer might have from one of the Police Department chaplains or the Medical Department.

Some public agencies have their own police, such as the New York Housing Authority, the New York Transit Authority, the Port of New York Authority. Some police work for the New York Central and Pennsylvania railroads, and privately for the Pinkerton and other private agencies. The actions of the police employed by such agencies is sometimes unjustly attributed to the members of the New York City Police Department, and when this was the case, referrals were made to the proper agencies.

Among the "cases referred" were the following:

A complaint alleged that a man driving on one of the parkways near New York was waved over to the curb by a man in another car. The other driver ordered, threatened, swerved, and forced the driver over to the curb. Then he showed a police shield and waved a gun and threatened to shoot. When the driver asked him to come along to the police station, the strange "policeman" drove away. Investigation of his car license brought out the fact that the "policeman" was a member of the railroad police of one of the main railroads with terminal facilities in New York. The complaint was referred to the railroad police of the appropriate railroad.

One complaint which required a great deal of time and energy on the part of the staff concerned an allegation of rape. It was alleged that the woman complainant had been waiting at a bus stop in the early morning. A car with four policemen had stopped and forced her into the car. They had taken her to a lonely section of the city and had raped her. Through the complainant's description of their physical characteristics and her description of the car and through inquiries in bars, it was possible to identify the individuals. They were members of one of the other police forces, not the police force of New York City. The case was turned over to the appropriate agency.

One complaint by a bystander:

> I wish to inform you of an incident of brutality on the part of several New York City policemen, which I witnessed on August 6, 1966, at 12:50 A.M., in the Jay Street–Boro Hall Station of the IND Subway in Brooklyn.
>
> I noticed a Negro man sitting handcuffed against the wall, refusing to speak to the five or six officers who surrounded him. He stood up and persisted in requesting a lawyer. The policemen began harassing him by telling him to "shut up" and by shoving him. Aware of my presence, two policemen pushed him around a corner. While I was still able to see him, one of them kicked him in the groin with his knee. I recorded one badge number but could not see the number of the officer who kicked him. Then a policeman told me and my friend to move along.
>
> The badge numbers are ________ and ________. The latter is the number of the officer who spoke to me.

> I realize that I do not have enough evidence, such as the victim's name to present a substantial legal case. However, circumstances did not permit me to approach the victim, since the officers' actions made it evident that they did not want me to interfere. I do not know why the victim was arrested, but there was no justification for the malicious and degrading treatment which he received. Nor was there justification for the insulting manner in which I was spoken to.

Investigation sometimes revealed that the shield numbers given by the complainant were those of policemen who at the time of the incident were on duty in precincts distant from the location of the alleged brutality. The complaint was sent on to the agency most likely to be involved. The shield numbers might be those of members of their police force.

Although the agencies employing police have some provision for dealing with complaints, the public has little knowledge of them. Nor is there anything like the same sense of accountability as is found in the administration and the General Order of the Police Department of New York City. When the Review Board referred cases to these agencies, there was no assurance that they were followed through with effective and impartial investigations and reviews and disciplinary action. Approximately five out of every hundred complaints had to be referred to other police agencies.

Unsubstantiated

When the allegation in a complaint lacked supporting evidence beyond a reasonable doubt, the complaint was classified as "unsubstantiated." The investigation of the allegation under a captain, the judgment of the complaint supervisor that the investigation had gone as far as it could, and the confirmation by the executive director—all this preceded the submission of the complaint to the Review Board members for individual study and collective discussion and disposition. If there simply was no supportive evidence or reliable witnesses upon which to base proof, the verdict was "unsubstantiated." In the number of complaints which came in each month, about half were found to be "unsubstantiated."

Some will deny, and some will find it hard to believe, that an able, impartial, and devoted investigating staff could not find truth in the allegations. But the fact is that many complainants, especially in the lower-income and less-literate groups of the populations, have never been educated to make a complaint or to realize that an allegation has to be backed with fact that can be established objectively. Witnesses or evidence of some sort must be available. Sometimes, even if there is some reason to believe the investigation will prove the validity of the complaint, the one person who might have helped may withdraw and become uncooperative or unavailable. Sometimes it is the one witness who "blows" and there is no case.

Many incidents occurred at night on the street with nobody near to act as witness. The police who usually traveled in twos tended to corroborate the statement of the officer or officers accused. In some cases, the complainant had a police record and this made it difficult to take his word against that of a police officer.

Occasionally the complainant was unclear or was under the influence of alcohol or narcotics or high emotional stress. In some instances the complainant withdrew his complaint. It was impossible to know whether he did this out of a "next morning sobering re-evaluation" or whether he had decided that it wasn't worth his time or that he should be more cautious in exposing himself to possible retaliation.

A commercial vehicle and a passenger car are in collision in the early-morning traffic. No one is injured. The passenger car is damaged. The operator of the car refuses to exchange driver's license and registration with the other driver until the police arrive. The two drivers argue. The police officer, when he arrives, is accused of being indifferent at first and then of using vile language. There are no witnesses to corroborate the complaint. If there are any, they do not come forward.

Complainant says he was sitting on the stoop in front of his dwelling place with a friend and that a policeman asked him for identification. He showed the officer his house key and mailbox key. He alleges that the officer ordered him to move, pushed him, and grabbed him by the neck and broke his metal neck chain. The officer claims that he used no physical force and that the man was intoxicated. In a line-up at the station house the complainant identified two patrolmen, at different times, contradicted himself, and then his friend denied the allegations of the complainant. In such circumstances the Review Board had no choice but to declare the complaint "unsubstantiated."

Two major questions must be in the mind of any persons (police or civilians) who presume to pass judgment on police behavior. *First,* is there evidence beyond any reasonable doubt that the police are guilty of the acts of which they are accused? This requires some confirmation: either admissions by the police or external evidence through witnesses and photographs, hospital records, etc. *Second,* a judgment as to whether in the given circumstances the actions of the police were reasonable and in accord with sound professional performance.

Some complaints were made because civilians did not know the law. Some did not know the responsibilities of the police and what it was reasonable to expect. A police officer on special assignment or called in emergency may not be able to do what a civilian demands.

When the Review Board members thought that the

disposal of a case as "unsubstantiated" might not do justice to the complainant because there were still some unresolved questions, the Review Board had two possible courses of action: it could return the case to the staff for further investigation or it could recommend a hearing. The first course usually grew out of the Board request for answers to specific questions and the hope that investigation might uncover a few more crucial facts. The hearing was held with the hope that it would uncover some new evidence or provide a basis for judging the credibility of the parties. Both recourses were considered where the allegations were serious and where there was reason to believe that injury and injustice had been done.

Of the cases which were not classified as "unsubstantiated" there were many where the complainant was correct in his basic facts but ignorant of the law or was mistaken in his understanding of police responsibility. It was characteristic of former police review boards to throw out such cases as if they were "unsubstantiated." But it is precisely such cases which include many of the misunderstandings and conflicts between people and police. And it was in recognition of the importance of such cases that General Order No. 14 provided for conciliation. This classification, which enabled the Review Board to refer cases in ways which would respect facts and feelings and clarify the mutual rights and responsibilities of civilians and police, was a new and valuable approach to dealing with a substantial number of complaints.

It should be pointed out that when the Review Board

found the complaint unsubstantiated, a letter went to the complainant.

A letter would go also to the officer informing him of this finding and reporting to him that there would be no record of the complaint in his professional police folder.

Conciliation

A unique feature of the Review Board in New York in 1966 was the provision for conciliation. Cases referred for conciliation were those in which there was no serious dispute on the facts. The differences might rest on the interpretation of the facts. A civilian might see an incident and the policeman's behavior one way. The policeman's job and his responsibility might make for a quite different way of dealing with the same incident. Difference of viewpoint might account for the misunderstanding and criticism and conflict.

The purpose of conciliating the case was to bring each party to an understanding that there might be some justification for the viewpoint and behavior of the other. Conciliation rested on the assumption that there might be mistakes by the police which might merit some explanation and criticism. Out of the effort to conciliate the cases in this category the police might learn from their mistakes and improve their performance. They might be more sensitive to public reactions.

The Review Board and staff held joint discussions so that the Review Board would be clear on which cases should be referred to conciliation and so that the conciliation officer would be clear on his functions and responsibilities. Everyone was aware that the effective working of the conciliation feature of the Civilian Complaint Review Board could be a significant contribution to better relationships between the people and the police. But they were also aware that conciliation required sensitivity and tact and genuine consideration for the complainant who thought he was wrongly dealt with and the police officer who probably thought he was right in what he had done and might be under the strain and anxiety of having a complaint made against him. Ideally, where wrong was done on both sides and misunderstandings had resulted, a meeting of the parties and a discussion might result in understanding and mutual regrets or apologies.

But what of the cases where the police officers had conducted themselves properly and had done their duty well? If the complaint was due to civilian ignorance of the law or a misunderstanding of the responsibilities of the police, the complainant was called in and informed and educated concerning the law and police duties. He might be quite satisfied with the explanation and grateful for the attention to his complaint. The police officer would be told that the complaint was unsubstantiated.

What of the case where the police officer had been guilty of neglect or mistaken action, where the officer had been at fault but where the injury was minimal? The civilian would know that a mistake had been made, that his complaint had been given attention, and that efforts would be made to assure that the mistake would not be repeated. In some cases a joint confrontation and reconciliation might be feasible and desirable.

The decision whether complainant and respondent should be brought together or dealt with separately was left to the discretion of the conciliation officer and the executive director. In some cases it was felt one or more Board members might participate helpfully in the conciliation process but this was left to the discretion of the deputy director.

A well-dressed and well-educated Negro woman approaches a young white policeman on duty in Times Square. "Officer," she says, "I need your help. I just bought this transistor radio and now it doesn't work. Will you accompany me to the store and help me get it repaired or get me a new one or get my money back?"

"Lady, only suckers buy things like that in Times Square."

"But Officer, I need your help."

"Lady, I got other things to do. Besides, your beef is not in my jurisdiction. It belongs in a civil court."

The woman complains that the officer was negligent and used derogatory language. Possibly she thought he acted as he did because she was Negro. Possibly she didn't understand his assignment in Times Square and that he couldn't leave his post to tend to her personal matter.

A doctor calls a policeman at 47th Street and Sixth Avenue to come to the aid of a man who is stricken in the street two blocks away. The policeman is on a special beat covering the diamond market. He is torn by the call for help and the possibility that this could be a decoy to draw him away. The officer finally leaves his post and when he sees the stricken man, he goes into a shop for an ambulance. The complainant charges delay in the officer's response and charges that the officer could have saved time if he had used the public telephones in the street. The civilian complainant in this case knows nothing about the special assignment of the officer and he does not know that experience has taught the officer that he will get quicker service from the store telephone, which is less likely to be out of order from vandalism, than the public phone.

In another case, a Negro is sitting in a car, writing on some slips of paper. The police officers observing from the patrol car decide to stop him and search him and bring him in. They arrest him for having policy slips. He turns out to be of Puerto Rican background and literally does not know what "policy" means. He is a delivery man and he is going over his delivery slips at the time. When the officers are confronted with the fact and the endorsement of the man's employer and the witnesses to his character they are ready to apologize.

In still another case a Negro man complains: "I want this boy locked up for burglary."

White officer: "Are you sure it's burglary? According to the law burglary means illegal entry. Are you sure it was illegal entry? Do you know this boy?"

"Yes, I know him. I told him to stay away from my daughter."

"She let him in, didn't she?"

"I want him arrested for burglary."

"Look, man, we can't do that. You can't prove it." Complaint allegation is discrimination.

A Negro from Virginia is driving late at night on the Queens parkway. An officer stops him and orders him to pull over to the side. The officer demands his driver's license and registration. The Negro asks, "Why did you stop me?"

The police officer says, "I don't need to answer your questions, hand me your driver's license and your registration."

The Negro says, "I'm entitled to know why you stopped me, what the charges are against me, and I will not hand over my driver's license or registration until you tell me."

"Since you won't hand over your registration or driver's license," says the officer, "I don't know whether you have the right to drive or whether this is your car or a stolen car. I'll have to drive you in, move over."

The police officer drives the car to the precinct house and just before he is about to make the arrest the man hands over his driver's license and registration. Meanwhile the car has been searched and nothing illegal has been found in the compartment or the trunk. The accused charges false search and false arrest.

The complainant thought he was being stopped because he was Negro. His experiences in the South had led him to believe that the police are always prejudiced against Negroes and violate their rights. He does not know that the police officer has the right to stop him and that on that particular evening he had been directed to stop cars on that parkway for specific offences. The offence for which the Negro was stopped was "weaving." Indeed, the officer in question had given out four summonses to white persons for weaving that evening. Furthermore, it is a regulation in the Police Department that any car taken into possession should be searched. The officer has no choice in the matter. But when the man asked to know what the charges were against him the officer might have saved a great deal of trouble by explaining that he had stopped him for weaving. On the other hand, if the man had handed over his driver's license and registration, he might have avoided a great deal of trouble, especially being forced to move over and be driven to the police station. Neither party had done anything seriously wrong. It seemed to the Review Board that here was a case for conciliation where explanations might be given which would help the Negro see that he was not the victim of discriminatory action. Also, the officer with a little more courtesy and a frank answer to the question might have avoided the unpleasantness of a complaint.

Conciliation procedure had the advantage of affording an opportunity to educate the complainant and to help the police face the reactions of the public to their conduct. For the police officer who was called to account, the effectiveness of the method depended in good part on the personality and tact of the conciliation officer. In some instances where the police officer had made a mistake the case was referred to his immediate superior on the precinct level so that he might benefit by discussion and instruction from a member of the police force with whom he worked most closely.

Conciliation could work only where the complainant was cooperative. Where he was in error and refused to accept the fact that his complaint rested on ignorance of the law or misunderstanding of the responsibilities of the police or where his allegations could not be proved true, the case had to be disposed of as "unsubstantiated."

When a case was conciliated, a letter was sent to the police officer to this effect as well as to the civilian complainant. It was made clear to the officer that, just as in the case of complaints which were "unsubstantiated," there would be no record of the complaint in his career folder. Where civilian ignorance or misunderstanding or false allegations constituted a substantial part of the basis for the complaint, these would not be entered in an officer's record.

On the other hand, if in the course of the investigation or the conciliation process it became evident that serious misconduct was involved, serious misuse of force or abuse of authority or corruption or serious injury, facts that might be to the detriment of the officer, the conciliation procedure was broken off and the report sent to the executive director for further investigation or hearings.

As the work of the Review Board proceeded, the conciliation officer reported that in many of the conciliation cases the complainants were anxious to discuss personal matters unrelated to the incident on which the complaint was made and were pleased that the Police Department provided someone who served as a willing listener. He concluded that the conciliation service was of great value to the community relations of the Police Department. It gave people a sense that the Department respected and listened to civilian problems.

In more than one case which was recommended for conciliation, the conciliation officer was able to report that the complainant "stated that he was pleased that I had called and also stated that he was certainly willing to settle the matter informally. He was happy to know that someone had taken a real interest in his case from the Civilian Complaint Review Board, but that he did not have any animosity at the present time toward the police officers. He thanked me and stated that he was 'pleased with the action that has resulted in this matter.' Accordingly, a letter of informal settlement was sent to the complainant."

It is important to note that if the investigation and review found that the case should be referred for "conciliation" or "hearings," this in no way affected the obligation of the complainant to meet his duty to respond to the summons or face the consequences of the arrest in the courts of law.

Hearings

Cases were referred for hearings when the Review Board found that the staff investigations still left critically important questions unanswered and when there were clear contradictions in the stories of the complainant and the policeman. Cases were referred for hearings where there seemed to be reason to believe that there might be some truth in the complainant's allegations, where witnesses might throw some light on the case, and where direct observation of the complainant and the policeman testifying under oath and subject to cross-examination might afford an opportunity to make a judgment on the credibility of the parties and of the witnesses. If the complaint alleged serious misconduct such as brutality and if the case was of particular community significance, this was also a reason to consider hearing the case so that no one could possibly hold that the complaint had not been given full consideration.

At the suggestions of the hearing officers and the executive director the Review Board discussed the regulations which might assure effective and fair procedures. Under the old Review Board consisting of police members only the civilian complainant was at a distinct disadvantage. If he had no attorney or witnesses, he might be sitting alone surrounded by police. If he was Negro or Puerto Rican, if he was a person lacking in education or unfamiliar with the English language, he might have little chance to substantiate his allegations. Often he had no familiarity with the procedures of a hearing and lacked the ability and skill to deal with establishing evidence and coping with cross-examination. The Review Board and staff members recognized the requirements of effective and fair hearings and made the following provisions:

The hearings were to be formal and dignified. At the same time every possible effort would be made to create a relaxed atmosphere and put the complainant and the respondent at ease. The atmosphere was not that of a court or an adversary proceeding. The hearing was treated as an extension of the investigation of the case to achieve a finding of facts beyond. The following rules of procedure were a development of the basic regulations provided for in General Order No. 14. They were undertaken after clearance with the Department of Legal Affairs of the Police Department and after consultation with the counsel of the Patrolman's Benevolent Association:

1. The place of hearings shall be at the offices of the Civilian Complaint Review Board, unless otherwise directed by the Executive Director.
2. Hearings shall be conducted by Hearing Officers of the Civilian Complaint Review Board.

3. The Board or the Chairman if the Board delegates such power to the Chairman, may designate one member of the Board appointed by the Mayor to represent the Board at such hearing or may designate for such purpose a panel of three, five or seven Board members so long as the majority of each such panel shall consist of members appointed by the Mayor.

4. The time of the hearing shall be fixed by the Hearing Officer upon reasonable notice to the interested parties. Hearings shall be completed as soon as possible.

5. Copies of U.F. 245 (Civilian Complaint Report) and U.F. 246 (Statement of Witness) filed in the case, and the Rules of Procedure Governing the Hearings, shall be furnished the member or members of the Police Department complained of and the complainant at least one week prior to the time of the hearings.

6. The Police Commissioner may, in his discretion, issue subpoenas to compel the attendance at hearings or the production of evidence upon the request of:

(a) any member of the Board representing the Board at the hearing
(b) The Hearing Officer
(c) the complainant, if approved by the Hearing Officer
(d) the member complained of, if approved by the Hearing Officer.

Upon receipt of notice of hearing, any complainant or member complained of desiring the issuance of a subpoena shall make his request promptly to the Hearing Officer.

7. The testimony taken at the hearings shall be under oath.

8. An interpreter shall be provided by the Board at the hearing if the services of an interpreter are deemed desirable in the discretion of the Hearing Officer.

9. If the complainant or any member or members complained of is financially unable to hire counsel, the Board shall assist in arranging such representation. Examination and cross-examination by the attorney for the complainant or the member or members complained of shall be permitted. A member or members complained of or the complainant may examine or cross-examine if not represented by an attorney.

10. Hearings shall not be open to the public. The complainant, the member or members complained of, and their respective lawyers and/or representatives may be present throughout the entire hearings. The number of representatives shall not be unreasonable and may be limited by the Hearing Officer conducting the hearing, or the Executive Director, in their discretion.

11. Rules of evidence shall not be applied strictly as in courts of law or equity, but shall be followed generally by the Hearing Officer to the end that the record of testimony transcribed at the hearing shall be as complete, relevant and accurate as possible. The Hearing Officer shall rule on the relevancy of questions.

12. A transcript shall be made of the testimony taken at each hearing. Any person who testifies at a hearing shall have an opportunity to review the transcript of his testimony at the offices of the Board, subject to the Rules of the Board. Any

member of the Police Department complained of, or the complainant, shall be allowed to purchase a copy of the transcript upon request to the Executive Director.

OPENING STATEMENT AT HEARINGS
to be made by the Hearing Officer.

This is a hearing set down by the Civilian Complaint Review Board in the matter of the complaint of __________ against __________, of the New York City Police Department. This complaint is designated as Serial No. ________, the substance of which is as follows:

The purpose of the hearing is to learn all the facts with respect to the complaint so that a fair and impartial determination may be made. All the witnesses are requested to testify to their best recollection of what they saw and heard and know as to the facts relevant to the complaint. Please do not tell us of rumors or gossip or what you may have imagined, as this will not help us get the facts. The method we use to get the facts is to ask questions; *first, your attorney will ask you* questions, then the *attorney for the person complained against* will ask you questions, and then, possibly, *I will* ask you some questions. Whenever objection is made to any question asked of you, I will make a ruling, and if I rule that the question is not a proper one, you need not answer it. It is our uniform procedure that all testimony at these hearings be given under oath and taken down by a stenographer.

Now for the record I will identify the parties present. My name is __________, and I am the Hearing Officer designated by the Board to conduct this hearing. On my right is Mr. ________, a member of the Board who is representing the Board at this hearing. (Then continue to identify remaining persons in the hearing room.)

Mark for identification the Notice of Hearing (which normally would transmit copies of U.F. 245 (Civilian Complaint Report), and U.F. 246 (Statement of Witness) and Rules of Procedure governing hearings). Confirm in the record that copies of the foregoing were received by complainant and member complained of at least one week prior to the hearings.

Swear in the first witness and begin taking testimony.

N. B. The foregoing is intended as a guideline where counsel for both sides is present. Where no attorney is present for one or the other party, the Hearing Officer will expand the opening statement to cover, among other things, the following:

1. That the party himself may ask questions.
2. That the Hearing Officer will lend either party who is without counsel assistance in asking questions.
3. That a recess may be had whenever necessary.

The following cases are examples of the type of complaint that have been referred for hearing and some of the problems involved:

One case which involved the arrest of five young Puerto Rican teenagers for an alleged theft (of which they may well have been guilty) necessitated a line-up of police so that the teenagers could identify them. The arrest had been made by a decoy method by members of the Tactical Force working in a neighborhood with a high incidence of mugging and theft. The complaint was made by the oldest of the young men. He alleged that he had been beaten when apprehended and while being taken in the patrol car from the scene of the arrest to the precinct station house. Either he refused to answer questions or he was fresh to the police or he refused to be silent when ordered. According to his complaint, he was struck about the legs and on the face with a gun or blackjack or club. His jaw was broken. He was hospitalized and there was a hospital record of his injury.

The case was reviewed and referred for hearing. The final determination of the case could not be completed before the termination of the Review Board by the Referendum of November 8, 1966. Subsequently the complainant was convicted. He withdrew the complaint. The policy of continuing the investigation and review even if the complaint is withdrawn is essential to the effective operation of the Review Board and the correction of police misconduct. The question is who broke the man's jaw? If the young man had an accident and if the hospital record shows the date to be before the incident, then the police are cleared. If one of the police did use unnecessary force and broke the complainant's jaw or if he beat him as alleged, then for the sake of other civilians and the future career of this policeman the matter had better be cleared up. But when a complainant goes off to prison and witnesses are uncooperative, further investigation is impossible.

An example of a complaint filed by a bystander involved a man who came out on his terrace overlooking the street late on a summer evening. What the bystander saw in the street below led him to make the complaint of police brutality by white police against a Negro. He alleged that two white policemen held a young Negro while a civilian lit a match in the boy's face and struck him. He alleged that the young Negro cried out for help.

At the first session of the hearing the young Negro who had been arrested and allegedly beaten was not present. He had been let out on bail and could not be reached. It was reported that he was out of town and that his trial would take place within a few weeks. The complainant, the bystander, was present with his attorney provided by the American Civil Liberties Union. The plain-clothes man from the Narcotics Squad and the two police officers who had been accused of holding the victim were present and aided by an attorney provided by the Patrolmen's Benevolent Association. The Narcotics man testified that he had been observing the suspect for some time and had seen him engage in narcotics deals on three occasions. When he had moved in for an arrest, he had asked the two men on the beat to assist him. The young man was searched, the paper with the white powder was found. When one of the assisting officers held a flashlight as the paper was opened, the suspect blew the powder away and tried to break away. It was at this point that he and the two officers grabbed the suspect. From the balcony about thirty feet above the street and in the ten-o'clock darkness of the night it might have seemed that a match was lit in the suspect's face, and from the quick move of the police it might have appeared that the suspect was being beaten, but the testimony of the police denied the allegation of brutality.

Both the complainant and the police were subjected to cross-examination. The hearing proceedings were recorded. The record would have to wait for a second session when the alleged victim of the beating would, hopefully, be present. Because of the absence of the accused and the postponed trial date and the Referendum in which the Review Board was terminated, it is not possible to report the final decision.

Charges

When the investigation indicated that the complaint had substance and that the police behavior fell within the C.C.R.B. jurisdiction, charges were sent on to the police commissioner. The Review Board made no recommendations of specific disciplinary measures. It was within the authority of the police commissioner to decide what disciplinary action should be taken. Thus the Board was an agency for receiving complaints from the people for investigating and fact finding and for recommendations and advice to the police commissioner. In the following cases the Review Board found the allegations to be true and recommended "charges."

Two police officers responded to a communications call from a woman who telephoned that three Negroes were burglarizing an apartment on a floor of her apartment house. The policemen charged up to the floor, banged on the door, called out, "Open up. Police!" When no one opened, one police officer shot the lock out of the door. Then both kicked in the door and the second officer charged in, shooting in all directions. The two police found two Negroes lying flat on the floor and one hiding in a closet. Had the two men not fallen flat and had the one in the closet not climbed on a shelf and hugged the wall, there would have been a killing. Photographs revealed the bullet holes at chest height. Search of the apartment revealed no weapons or narcotics or stolen goods. The three Negroes belonged there. It was their apartment. The breaking in and the use of the guns occasioned a complaint of unnecessary use of force, illegal entry and search, and the destruction of property.

An off-duty policeman out of uniform attempts to shut off a hydrant where children had been wading and bathing in the street in a Negro area of one of the boroughs. After he turns off the hydrant, he warns the boys not to turn it on. When he walks away, they start toward the hydrant again. The off-duty police officer then takes out a blackjack and goes after the boys, mostly of junior high-school age. While he pokes or hits them, a girl rushes into the street and stands between the stranger and her little brother. She argues and fights with him. Up to this point no one has any idea that the man is a police officer. He picks up this young woman, throws her down on the street, and breaks her nose and lacerates her face. As the crowd gathers, the man reveals to a Housing Authority police officer that he is a policeman. *Then he proceeds to arrest the young woman . . . on the charge of interfering with an officer, etc.* The young woman is a nurse at a city hospital and quite properly defended her little brother against what appeared to be a sadistic and officious unknown civilian. The finding of the Review Board was brutality and false arrest.

The Use of Force

When the community delegates authority to a police force, it expects force to be used where it is necessary for the protection of persons and property and public order. Just as police should not use unnecessary force in law enforcement, so they should not refrain from using it to the extent that it is necessary.

What force is necessary for the restraint or the apprehension and arrest or the recapture of the alleged offender?

One form of advice would be "never use a hand where a word will do, or a club where a hand will do, or a gun where a club will do. Never strike with thirty pounds of weight where ten pounds will do. Never strike three times where once will do." Is this an adequate guide for action?

One form of what people mean by "police brutality" is the "third degree." This has meant beatings or torture to break a person's will so that he will answer questions or give the answers desired or confess to a crime. Even as late as the 1940s the third degree was accepted police practice in the city of New York. The incoherent drunk, the homeless man on the Bowery, the Negro or other minority-group member might be picked up as a suspect and given the third degree. Police Commissioner Lewis Valentine and even Mayor LaGuardia resisted the increased publicity and the criticism of the practice. The general public, the law-abiding, respectable, churchgoing members of the community scarcely raised their eyebrows or uttered one voice of denunciation.

According to U.S. Civil Rights Commission Report of 1961:

> In 1931 President Hoover's Wickersham Committee found extensive evidence of police lawlessness including unjustified violence. Sixteen years later another Presidential Committee, this one appointed by President Truman, concluded that police brutality, especially against the unpopular, the weak, and the defenseless, was a distressing problem. And now in 1961 this Commission must report that police brutality is still a serious problem throughout the United States.

"Police brutality" is a slogan raised to cover a multitude of evils: unnecessarily to lay hands on an individual who is cooperating with a police command; to "rough up" a person who is in custody and constitutes no threat to police operation; to use a club or blackjack or gun or handcuffs when these are not necessary. "Brutality" means killing, beating, pushing, pulling, dragging, striking, and it may mean holding, restraining, putting on handcuffs, when these are not necessary for the enforcement of the law in particular situations.

When people cry police brutality in the first instance

they mean physical mistreatment which inflicts injury or death. By brutality they also mean the equivalent of what we call in war an atrocity, that is the infliction of an injury or death on persons already subdued or already in custody where there was no resistance at all or only nonviolent resistance, or where if there was resistance it has been overcome. An atrocity is clearly an injury done out of fear or hate or uncontrollable sadistic impulse.

The charge of "unnecessary use of force" or "excessive use of force" is not a simple matter. For an unbiased judgment on police action a number of factors have to be taken into account and one has to ask in each case, What is it reasonable to expect of the police? What is good professional practice?

Most of the complaints alleging physical brutality are hard to substantiate. Where there are no witnesses and no marks of physical injury or medical record, and where there is bias against or for the police, the facts are hard to come by. Yet with honest and expert investigation and thorough checking it is possible to get at the truth a certain percentage of the time. Where investigation leaves certain questions unanswered, a hearing may settle matters beyond a reasonable doubt and establish the credibility of the complainant and the officer concerned.

A few specific cases illustrate some of the problems of the Civilian Complaint Review Board:

A wife attending a holiday parade is separated from her husband. While standing looking for him, she is told to move by a police officer. He is unnecessarily rude. She moves but not enough to satisfy him. He is rude again, and this time he puts his hands on her and shoves her into the crowd. She is seven months along in her pregnancy and frightened. After the complaint is brought, the officer denies the allegations of the unnecessary use of force and discourtesy. She cannot find any witnesses to help her. Should the complaint be declared "unsubstantiated" or referred for "conciliation"?

A complainant alleges that he was thrown out of a restaurant by a policeman. He had been drinking there and then had gone to another bar nearby. There he remembered that he had left his briefcase in the first restaurant. He returned to find it. He claims that while he was there looking for it a policeman who was eating lunch stood up and threw him out, pushing and shoving him into the street. According to the police officer and the witnesses the man had come into the bar, had disturbed everyone, and abused the police officer. Finally, he had been urged to leave and then taken by the arm gently but firmly and escorted to the door. The complainant withdrew his complaint the next morning with the remark that he knew he had been drunk. Numerous witnesses testified that the man was escorted gently and without "brutality" or undue use of force.

A man on a bus, under the influence of alcohol, abused the driver and disturbed the passengers by his profanity and his behavior. The bus driver stopped the bus, phoned the police, and asked that the man be removed. The police tried to eject the man. The complainant held on to the railing and benches of the bus in his effort to resist the police. He was removed. He charges unnecessary use of force. Passengers witnessing the action testify that there was no roughness whatever.

Some of the complaints about police brutality come not from victims but from bystanders. An example is a complaint alleging that brutality was committed by five policemen against a single individual in the early-morning hours in front of a nightclub. The bystander saw the unknown swing at one of the policemen after an argument. The police officer then grabbed him. Both fell to the ground. The other four policemen joined in the struggle. One put his knee on the young man's body. Another snapped on the handcuffs. Then they lifted the young man and "threw him into a taxi." Two of the policemen then took him away. The finding of fact is that the young man had drunk too much and was put out of the tavern by the bouncer. When the victim appealed to the police to be readmitted to the tavern, he was given no sympathy. He swung at one of the policemen. Hence the arrest and charge of assaulting a policeman. When interviewed on the complaint, the young man admitted that he was intoxicated. He himself did not complain of police brutality and unnecessary use of force.

Many police tend to assume that they have the right and even the duty to use force when their authority is challenged or they are treated with disrespect. If a suspect or an alleged lawbreaker or a prisoner gets "smart" or resists questioning or refuses to give the answers or admissions they want, the police often get rough and feel that it is justified. But a teacher may not use force and violence against students or a social worker against clients just because they are difficult or insulting or threatening. Prison guards are not acting as professionals if they beat or torture those who are in their care. A nurse, doctor, psychiatrist, must sometimes stand much abuse from patients without violating the patient's rights. At their best, the police know and practice restraint no matter what insults and name-calling and threats come their way from individuals, gangs, or demonstrators. It is part of their job to "take it."

In another case, a nineteen-year-old was stopped by a traffic policeman. When he showed his car registration and license, he used some foul language and wanted to know what the charge was against him. The officer in anger struck him on the thigh with his nightstick. It is hard to understand why the officer did this, but investigation of the case showed that there was no dispute of this fact.

When a police officer orders a cessation of lawless behavior or desires cooperation, how can he assure it with safety to himself and effective compliance with his order? He may use words and a tone which are adequate to restrain or bring about compliance. But at what point is it reasonable for him to lay his hands on another person or use physical force? And if voice and hand prove inadequate, at what point is he justified in using a club or a gun or putting on handcuffs?

A woman complained that she was made to move from a street corner, was cursed, insulted, and beaten when she asserted her rights, and then was subjected to false arrest.

What is the true story? The officer told a group of women who were standing on a street corner to move along. Were they blocking traffic or causing a disturbance or committing a crime? No. The answer was that this corner is known as a hangout where prostitutes solicit. In the precinct this corner is one which is supposed to be kept clear by the officer on the beat. Thus the officer was following policy and instructions when he told the women to move on. All complied except one. She was Spanish-speaking, a known prostitute with past convictions. She refused to move. She spat at the officer and flipped her cigarette in his face. He took hold of her, and she fought. He beat her with his club and finally forced her into the patrol car. At the precinct house it was evident that she needed medical aid. He then drove her to Harlem Hospital. She may have cursed him on the way. She accused him of beating her on the legs during the ride in the car. On the way into the hospital she still fought and he still beat her. The complaint charged physical beating supported by written testimony from three hospital orderlies who watched from the hospital window and by the examining doctor who saw the effects. The medical report revealed lacerated scalp requiring six stitches, black eyes, and black-and-blue marks and bruises on legs and arms.

Admitting that this woman was a prostitute, was the officer correct in trying to force her to move? What rights on the street has she before she commits an infraction of the law? And if and when she refused to move, was he correct in his threat to arrest her? Was he correct in using force to put her in his car? Should he have beaten her?

These questions have to be answered from the viewpoint of civilian rights. What are the limits to the police power when a person who has a record and is a known past offender stands in the street but at the moment has committed no crime? If a woman is a lawbreaker, even a prostitute, does this justify this kind of beating? Can the officer's defense that she refused to move, that she insulted him and cursed him, that she spat or flipped her cigarette at him, justify his use of extreme force?

Had he no alternatives? Couldn't he have prevented soliciting by taking up his post on the corner? Or should he have called the precinct for assistance? With the help of another officer might he not have been able to subdue her without lacerating her scalp or beating her black and blue and until she bled?

When a policeman responds to an emergency call he is tense. Many things run through his mind while he is on the "run" to the scene of the crime—when he enters a bar or a dark alley, when he knocks on the door of an apartment and waits, not knowing what is on the other side. If the call is one involving a fight, and even more if the call indicates that there is a gun involved, he knows he is coming into a dangerous situation. He has to be ready to draw his gun; to take cover. He has to be ready to make a split-second decision. His life and the welfare of his wife and children are involved. He may take a chance and pay with his life. He may decide to shoot as the only safe way. In some situations his act may trigger a riot. He may also injure or kill an innocent man or a lawbreaker needlessly. If he is right he may be a hero and be promoted. If he is wrong, he may be brought up on complaints and disciplined severely.

The gun is a problem. The policeman mustn't let anyone get his hands on it. If he does, he may be killed. If a man is coming at him with a knife or a hammer or some other weapon, he should use it. And if he uses it, he may shoot to incapacitate the attacker. He knows that a hand gun lacks the power of a rifle or shotgun. It may not even stop a man or knock him down. Yet it is his only hope of safety if he is attacked. And if he doesn't draw his gun and use it (and survives), the higher-ups will want to know why. He may say, "I didn't think I needed to use it." Or he may say, "I didn't have it on me." In either case he is in trouble.

Some civilian complaints charged the unnecessary use of force. They referred to the fact that the police officer drew his gun in a situation where the complainants thought the use of a gun or deadly force was not called for. In a few of the situations which came to the Review Board's attention the danger stemming from the gun might have meant serious injury or death to a person who had not committed a crime. But besides the danger to the life of the individual suspect there is need for protection of innocent men, women, and children from the danger of bullets which scatter and ricochet.

A policeman trying to apprehend a participant in a crap game draws his gun, and as the participants scatter in flight, he shoots. The episode takes place in a neighborhood which is extremely tense and hostile to the police and could easily be triggered into a riot. The young man, a Puerto Rican, is hit in the thigh. Had the shot killed him, the consequences would have raised the question whether the use of a gun in such a case was justified. The Review Board recommended that the Police Department review its regulations on the use of firearms.

In the heat of summer a young patrolman is turning off the fire hydrant in a crowded Negro neighborhood. The children are taunting and teasing him, the young girls are joking. The old people are watching. The patrolman slips and falls in the puddles in the street. The crowd laughs. The patrolman loses his temper. In anger he draws his gun, threatens the crowd and orders them to disperse.

Police cars arrive. People scatter. A coke bottle is tossed into a police car. One of the officers jumps out of the car and, with gun drawn, chases after a boy who is running through the crowded open spaces around the housing project.

A teenager steals a car. The policeman is in pursuit. He draws his gun—shoots, and kills. Which weighs more in the balance? A boy's life or a car? Was this the only way to catch the teenager? Is this the best way to enforce the law? If the boy is fleeing, can it be said that the officer shot in self-defense? If a felony has been committed, is the gravity of the crime justification for shooting to kill?

Many police think that they are engaged in a war with crime. And to the extent that they think of it as war, they believe that anything goes. Thus a certain percentage use any means at hand and feel no compunction. They do not really expect society to inhibit them in the name of citizen rights. Many are convinced that the only language the lawbreaker understands is the business end of a club or a gun.

In the Police Academy shooting range, where police learn how to use firearms, the police officer graduates from practice shooting at a regular target to a target which is the shape of a man. The bull's-eye is in the middle of the man. Those who are being instructed are not taught to shoot at an arm or a leg. When questioned on this matter, the instructor says, "When the officer draws a gun he is supposed to use it. When he uses it, he is supposed to incapacitate completely the person who is threatening. If he shoots at an arm or leg, he may miss, if he shoots at the middle, he has a much better chance of hitting. Furthermore, if he hits a man in the middle he'll get total incapacitation." Then defensively the instructor said, "Not everybody who gets hit in the middle, in the abdomen, necessarily dies. Modern medicine can save him."

The gun is a responsibility and a temptation. It is a "deadly force." It should be a weapon of last resort. Instruction of police has usually taught that the gun should be drawn only if necessary and if drawn it should be used, and if used it should be used to incapacitiate even if this means to kill.

Every precinct has its peculiar atmosphere, its trouble spots, and local "characters"—unemployed, actors, natural comedians, local bosses, disturbed people, the harmless ones, and the troublemakers. An officer from outside the precinct or new to the area can make a serious mistake if he acts without knowing who or what he is dealing with:

A police officer driving up an avenue in a district other than his own sees a Negro speaking, singing, and brandishing a butcher knife. The crowd gathered around him is watching and listening, teasing him and enjoying the show. When he advances toward them, they back away. Unaware that this is a local "character," known to the precinct police as harmless as long as he is not threatened, the police officer thinks this is a case calling for emergency action. He stops his car, jumps out, draws his gun, and advances toward the man, saying, "Drop that knife!" The crowd, which had felt no danger, now withdraws. The man turns toward the officer and waves his knife. He may still be in a dramatic and playful mood. But this is a white man and a policeman, who has his gun drawn and appears serious and menacing. "Drop that knife!" says the officer. As the Negro advances the officer backs away, still appealing to the man to drop the knife. Finally, when both have moved down the block and are near the curb, the officer utters a last warning and shoots. The Negro falls dead. Everyone who witnesses the incident knows that it is all a mistake, an unnecessary tragedy. Would the local precinct police have known how to ignore or handle the situation?

In the 1966 report of the President's Commission on

Law Enforcement and Administration of Justice, the section titled, "Task Force Report: The Police," on page 183, reads as follows:

USE OF FIREARMS TO APPREHEND OR ARREST SUSPECTS

Police use of firearms to apprehend suspects often strains community relations or even results in serious disturbances. For example, the San Francisco riot of 1966 started after a juvenile was shot and killed while fleeing from a stolen car. Severe tensions were aroused in Los Angeles during May 1966, after an officer's firearm accidentally discharged and killed a man who had refused to stop his automobile until it was forced to the curb. In St. Louis, disturbances began in September 1966 after police officers shot and killed a person who had his hands handcuffed behind him in a police car located in the courtyard of Police Headquarters. The police assert that the suspect threatened officers in the car with a tear gas pistol he had in his belt behind him which the officers had failed to find in a search earlier.

When studied objectively and unemotionally, particular uses of firearms by police officers are often unwarranted.

A study by an American Civil Liberties Union affiliate in a medium-sized city found that officers fired guns more than 300 times in a two-year period and over one-third were during automobile chases involving juveniles. An average of 240 persons per year were fatally injured by police between 1950 and 1960. The Michigan State study concluded that police officers often use guns indiscriminately and that this was due, in large part, to overemphasis of danger in police work. While the murder of a single police officer is a tragedy, as of 1955 the rate of total police fatalities while on duty (including accidents) was 33 fatalities per 100,000 officers, which was less than the rate of deaths on duty in mining (94), agriculture (55), construction (76), and transportation (44).

For example, a 1961 survey of Michigan police forces found that 27 out of 49 had no firearms policies. A survey in 1964, of 45 of the 51 American cities of over 250,000 population, found that 3 had no written firearms policy, and, while others had comprehensive policy statements, many were quite limited. For example, one simply prohibited warning shots, one instructed its officers to "exercise the greatest possible caution," and 10 urged officers to use "good judgment."

It is essential that all departments formulate written firearms policies which clearly limit their use to situations of strong and compelling need. A department should even place greater restrictions on their use than is legally required. Careful review of the comprehensive firearms use policies of several departments and discussions with police administrators indicate that these guidelines should control firearms use:

1. Deadly force should be restricted to the apprehension of perpetrators who, in the course of their crime, threatened the use of deadly force, or if the officer believes there is a substantial risk that the person whose arrest is sought will cause death or serious bodily harm if his apprehension is delayed. The use of firearms should be flatly prohibited in the apprehension of misdemeanants, since

the value of human life far outweighs the gravity of a misdemeanor.

2. Deadly force should never be used on mere suspicion that a crime, no matter how serious, was committed or that the person being pursued committed the crime. An officer should either have witnessed the crime or should have sufficient information to know, as a virtual certainty, that the suspect committed an offence for which the use of deadly force is permissible.

3. Officers should not be permitted to fire at felony suspects when lesser force could be used; when the officer believes that the suspect can be apprehended reasonably soon thereafter without the use of deadly force; or when there is any substantial danger to innocent bystanders. Although the requirement of using lesser force, when possible, is a legal rule, the other limitations are based on sound public policy. To risk the life of innocent persons for the purpose of apprehending a felon cannot be justified.

4. Officers should never use warning shots for any purpose. Warning shots endanger the lives of bystanders, and, in addition, may prompt a suspect to return the fire. Further, officers should never fire from a moving vehicle.

5. Officers should be allowed to use any necessary force, including deadly force, to protect themselves or other persons from death or serious injury. In such cases, it is immaterial whether the attacker has committed a serious felony, a misdemeanor, or any crime at all.

6. In order to enforce firearms use policies, department regulations should require a detailed written report on all discharges of firearms. All

> cases should be thoroughly investigated to determine whether the use of firearms was justified under the circumstances.
>
> If all departments formulated firearms use policies which include the above principles and these policies were consistently enforced, many of the tragic incidents which had a direct bearing upon community relations could have been avoided.

Legislation to implement these directives has been attacked by spokesmen for the police and certain sections of the community. In part, the public is panicked in its fear of crime. It wants protection. People would rather permit brutality and excessive use of force than protect human rights or assure restrained and discriminating use of arms. People forget that innocent people get hurt, and not just by those committing crimes. The public rationalizes that the victims of the police are probably no-good people anyway or they wouldn't be suspects. But the public forgets that when the police hurt people indiscriminately or ruthlessly, the injury to individuals is also damaging to the police, to law enforcement, and to the government itself.

"Brutality" is not confined to the police. It may be worse when they practice it. But it stems from the civilian population. There is a widespread brutality and violence in everyday relationships. The police know it. And sometimes they, too, complain.

A patrolman complains:

"Why don't you get wise? You know where the brutality comes from? It comes from the civilians. A gang of kids are playing the blocks around here. When a woman makes a telephone call from the public booth, they grab her purse. When a guy leaves a car unlocked, they get his cigarettes, anything lying loose in the car. They'd mug their own mothers. You want to be fair to them? They ain't fair to anybody.

"So a man who has been robbed grabs a kid and wants to smash him. I come over and stop him. Mind you! I'm stopping civilian brutality. The kid hasn't been arrested or tried or found guilty. This white guy is ready to smash in the face and skull of a junior high-school kid! For what? He took his cigarettes. So I interfere to prevent brutality. But when I do it—even when I stop the crime or delinquency, they think it's police brutality."

Off-duty Police

The number of complaint cases involving off-duty policemen was very high. In some months they constituted almost a fifth of the total. Many cases were reported in the press. Off-duty police cases are a problem in most of the major cities.

In New York City the off-duty policeman is required to carry his shield and his gun at all times and to be ready to take action in law enforcement when needed. This means that the policeman is *on duty* even when he is not on his beat and even when he is without an assignment. Indeed, he is never off duty. The rationale and argument for the regulation hold that this gives the community extra protection. First, the total number of police ready to act at any moment is substantially larger than it would be if two-thirds of the police force were to be unavailable. Second, the off-duty officer without his uniform on is often in situations where he can see and hear and be on the spot to deal with a crime being committed or planned. Third, unarmed, police would be unable to take emergency action and many would be killed. For example:

In a bar a holdup man lines up the patrons at gun point and empties their pockets and the cash drawer at the bar. One patron is making a telephone call. When he is attacked, he comes out with a gun in his hand. He shoots the holdup man and foils the robbery. He is an off-duty policeman.

The argument against the regulation requiring the carrying of a weapon and the readiness to take action if needed is based on the fact that an off-duty policeman may be drawn into a personal conflict. He may use his fighting skills or his weapon or authority to subdue his opponent. The other party may think he is dealing as an equal, with a fellow civilian. He may not know that he is in triple danger: first, his opponent has the advantage of physical conditioning and training in fighting skills; second, his opponent is armed with a deadly weapon; third, his opponent has the authority to arrest him. Finally, when officers arrive, they may line up with their off-duty colleague in corroboration against the civilian.

In case after case it is evident that after an off-duty police officer has become involved in conflict, he has sometimes engaged in a physical fight or drawn his gun and threatened to use it or has used it. Then he has identified himself as a policeman and made an arrest on charge of assault and battery or disturbance of the peace or disorderly conduct, etc. This last he has done to protect himself, for he knows when he thinks it over that if he gets into a fight and uses his police weapon or authority, he may be subject to a suit for damages or criminal charges or a complaint before the Civilian Complaint Review Board. By making charges and an arrest he hopes to avoid these or to put the other person in a difficult position. Examples of such actions are as follows:

A man is getting into his brother's car. He opens the car door on the street side. A passing car jams on its brakes but not in time to prevent damage. The man jumps out and shouts at the driver. He demands his registration and license. He offers to take him on in a fight. Then he identifies himself as a policeman and issues a summons.

A father complains. His son is hurt in a collision with the car of an off-duty policeman in civilian clothes. *The policeman immediately makes out a summons.* He uses bad language. The son has never been in trouble. He had a good record of military service. No medical assistance is offered. He is threatened with arrest.

The Review Board agreed that if an off-duty police officer acted in any way as a policeman, his behavior could quite properly be the subject of a civilian complaint before the Review Board. If he showed his shield or used his weapon or made charges and an arrest, he acted as a policeman and should be judged as such.

If he behaved as a civilian and at no point used his shield or weapon or identity or authority as a policeman, he was not subject to the jurisdiction of the Civilian Complaint Review Board. However, a complaint based only on the knowledge (as a relative or neighbor might know it) that he was a member of the police force might, under some circumstances, be referred to the chief inspector. Obviously if there were many complaints concerning the personal life of a policeman it might be of concern to the Police Department even though the man was an exemplary police officer. In such cases the referral might be made by the police members of the Review Board.

In a family quarrel an off-duty police officer called a relative an "S.O.B.," knocked him down, and held him down while he hit him. Since the off-duty policeman at no time during this quarrel used his shield or weapons or authority as a police officer, the Review Board felt that this case was not within the jurisdiction of the Board. It referred the case to the chief inspector for further investigation and action. The Board held that it was concerned with cases involving only the officers of the Police Department of the City of New York *when they are on duty* or *when they attempt a police action.* In the above case the officer acted in his private capacity as a citizen. If the Police Department, through its chief inspector, decided to take action, that was in his discretion.

Another complainant charges the use of excessive force in an altercation in which he was hit in the eye resulting in impairment of vision. Complainant is suing the patrolman for damages for personal injury. The investigation reveals that the complaint arose out of a family quarrel between two brothers-in-law, one of them an off-duty policeman. Passers-by had to separate the opposing parties. Since the patrolman at no time used his police authority or weapons or identification, the complaint is not within the jurisdiction of the Review Board and is being referred to the chief inspector.

The gun is a serious part of the problem for the officer off duty. When he gets home, what shall he do with it?

Where shall he hide it? He doesn't want his children to get at it. He doesn't want it stolen. He hides it in what he thinks is a safe place.

At a party how can an off-duty policeman conceal his weapon? How can he dance without it being evident? And how can he be sure that someone won't grab it in fun or for serious use?

If he goes to the beach, where shall he leave it when he gets into his swimming suit? He can't leave it in a public locker with any security. If he carries it with him to the beach, it is all too evident. He hides it in his swimming trunks, puts it in his wife's or girl friend's handbag—and they take turns swimming and watching the handbag.

There was the policeman who hid his gun in a wastebasket. He figured that no thief would look there. He went out to buy groceries, and when he returned it was gone. The maid had emptied the wastebasket into the refuse container in the hall. The janitor had collected the refuse and emptied it into the basket at the street corner. It took him time to find the janitor. Then he raced to the corner litter basket just in time to retrieve his gun before the Sanitation Department workers arrived.

There are 28,000 policeman in the New York City Police Department. Eight thousand live outside the city. Are they to be responsible for carrying weapons and enforcing law when they are outside the city limits? What if they break the law on the way to or from work? What if they get into brawls while off duty and outside the city? What if they do so while in the city limits?

Many complaints would never be made and many

lives would be saved if it were required that the policeman's gun be kept in the security of the officer's locker in the precinct station house when he is off duty.

A sizable number of complaints and serious damage suits in the courts originate in the actions of off-duty police. And many of these come about because of excessive drinking. The strain of the police job makes men seek relaxation and companionship after they have finished their tour of duty. Arguments and quarrels in bars and at parties account for much of the trouble that police get into when they are not on official assignment.

Many tragedies would be avoided if off-duty officers were under a rule which forbids them to enter a bar with a loaded gun or with any gun at all. The problem of the unnecessary use of force and the abuse of authority by off-duty police still remains to be faced by the police and the larger community.

The Use of Authority

In the crime stories the policeman always gets his man. In real life the police officer may arrest the wrong person. In real situations he must make a judgment according to the facts he has—and he may be wrong.

He must bring in the person who has committed a serious violation of the law. Whatever discretion an officer has in most violations, serious violations of the law give the officer no choice. But he must be sure to have the right person. If he has sufficient evidence to justify belief that a person is guilty, he can and must arrest.

In many situations the policeman may have to weigh a variety of factors, for the number of calls for help and serious need may be far exceeded by those calls which do not involve serious violations of the law. He should not bring in people for trivial offences that could have been settled without an arrest. Quarrels between a man and a wife, between a storekeeper and a customer, between men in a bar or between neighbors, would usually be better settled without an arrest. Thus a policeman may order people to move on, break up a gathering, or move a car. When they fail to obey or are "difficult," he may make an arrest on charges of resisting an officer, disturbing the peace, or causing a crowd to gather.

The examples offered in the following complaints illustrate the kind of allegations which were made to the Review Board.

Four complainants charged a violation of rights and the abuse of authority in the case of a group of church members who had just returned from a church outing to Bear Mountain Park. It was a July-Fourth picnic and the busses returned late. At about 8 P.M. many church members were standing on the corner and talking in small groups. The complainants charged that two police officers accosted them, arrested them for disturbing the peace, and roughed them up. The separate complaints charged false arrest and undue use of force.

An elderly woman from out of town, visiting New York, crossed Broadway against the light and was given a summons for jaywalking. By a series of circumstances this well-mannered and well-educated woman got into an argument with the officer and ended up spending the night in jail. Something wrong was said or done by somebody. No doubt stubbornness played a part. The allegation was derogatory language and undue use of authority.

Two women got into an argument over their children. The argument led to a fight. One hit the other with a stone. With both women shrieking and the injured woman retiring to her apartment, the husband of the almost blinded woman telephoned the police. The police decided to take both women to the police station. The complaint alleges that the police made the injured woman get out of bed and accompany them. The two families charge the police with undue use of authority, false arrest, and derogatory treatment.

The driver of a car differed with the police officer over the charge of speeding. The officer charged 52 miles per hour. The driver said he was doing between 42 and 45. The allegation was that the police officer said, "Wise guy, eh?" and then put down 72 miles per hour. It was also alleged that the man was taken into custody, no attorney was allowed, and that he was kept locked up all night.

Some people tend to think that unless a policeman is making arrests he isn't doing his job. Indeed, some think that a policeman is to be judged by the number of arrests he makes in a given period of time.

In some cities the police supervisors keep track of the number of arrests a patrolman makes and use the results to make a judgment on the extent to which he is on the job. In some police departments "arrest quotas" are the practice. The pressure to fulfill such quotas constitutes a pressure on the policeman and may result in injustice to the civilians who happen to come by when a policeman feels that he must "produce."

In the 1966 report of the President's Commission on Law Enforcement and Administration of Justice, in the section titled, "Task Force Report: The Police," the passage on "Arrest Quotas" reads:

> Police work is far too complicated and delicate a job to judge an officer's work or qualifications for promotion on the number of arrests he has made.

> Furthermore, arrest quotas, if they exist as either explicit requirements or implied expectations, can lead to improper activity by policemen. Patrolling officers have the complex and difficult responsibility of exercising their discretion based on the circumstances of the particular case. No part of this calculation should consist of the number of arrests the officer has made in comparison to a pre-established quota or expectation set by the department.

The police have unusual powers. Faced by the policeman's authority to arrest, the citizen is powerless. The problem is: How can the people police the police so that they respect and protect human rights?

Most of the provisions of the Bill of Rights have been incorporated by the Fourteenth Amendment so as to apply to state action:

> Fourth Amendment: The right of the people to be secure in their persons, houses, papers, and effects, against unreasonable searches and seizures, shall not be violated, and no warrants shall issue but upon probable cause, supported by oath or affirmation, and particularly describing the place to be searched, and the persons or things to be seized.
>
> Fifth Amendment: No person shall be . . . compelled in any criminal case to be a witness against himself, nor be deprived of life, liberty or property, without due process of law. . . .
>
> Sixth Amendment: In all criminal prosecutions, the accused shall enjoy the right to a speedy and public trial . . . and to be informed of the nature and cause of the accusation; to be confronted with

> the witnesses against him; to have compulsory process for obtaining witnesses in his favor, and to have the assistance of counsel for his defense.

For the most part the Amendments and the popular interpretations of the "due process clause" are taken to provide for a fair trial in a court. But "due process of law" also applies to the treatment of citizens by the police before they get to the courtroom. It applies equally on the way to the police station and in the period of custody by the police.

In the past the police were generally unregulated in deciding when to arrest and how to treat civilians. Recent Supreme Court decisions have made it clear that under the constitutional protection of the individual's rights, "due process" requires that if the police interrogate a person in their custody they must inform him of his right to remain silent and his right to the aid of counsel. Lawful interrogation requires respect for these rights by the police.

Widespread violations of constitutional rights by the police in many parts of the nation and appeals to the federal courts have resulted in the dismissal of cases in which convictions had rested upon evidence illegally obtained. Thus recent Supreme Court decisions now act as guiding principles for making certain that the people are protected from the abuse of police authority. If police are to assure that arrests will result in convictions, they must gather their evidence by methods in accord with the latest interpretations of "due process of law."

These recent court decisions are not only attempts to

protect the individual in his basic rights but also to protect the community from bad law enforcement. There is no safety for the community if the wrong man is convicted under pressure while the real lawbreaker goes free.

Complaints of abuse of authority or the excessive use of authority stem from false arrest and the accosting, detaining, and searching of citizens.

Many of the complaints have no relation to the treatment of members of minority groups, Negro or Puerto Rican. They have to do with the "stop and frisk" police actions against all people. The average American who is innocent of crime and is going about his own affairs prizes his freedom and his right to privacy. To be accosted in the street or a public place and to be asked to identify himself is needless interference with his freedom and his privacy. It may occasion inconvenience and delay. It may be embarrassing. Unless the police officer has a "probable cause" to believe that he has committed a crime, such restraint and detention are violations of the citizen's rights.

True, no rights and freedoms are absolute. But neither should such acts of lawless violations by the police be ignored or condoned. False arrest, search and seizure without warrant, harassment, the planting of incriminating evidence, coerced confessions or physical mistreatment of those detained, denial of access to a counsel—all these are intolerable to free men. They are not conducive to respect for the police or to good law enforcement.

"Stop" actions present problems for the police and the

public. Has the policeman the right to stop a citizen and ask his name and address? Has he the right to ask for identification or to ask the individual what he is doing at this particular location at this particular time?

Normally a citizen who is stopped by the police and asked his name and address is likely to cooperate. And if he is asked to accompany the police to the police station he may go along as an act of civic responsibility. But if he refuses to give his name and address, to stop for further questioning, or to accompany the policeman to the police station, he is within his constitutional rights. He may have made the police job more difficult by his unwillingness to cooperate, but he cannot be accused of willfully obstructing the police in the execution of their duty.

The question is a little more difficult where the policeman stops an individual not as a suspect but as a possible aid in giving information or as a witness so that the police can identify and catch the lawbreaker. Has the policeman the right to detain, question, or compel the individual to accompany him to the scene of the crime or to the police station? Or is the policeman's authority limited to a request for help and cooperation on a voluntary basis?

If the police arrest a man, they can compel him to accompany them. But they should tell him of the charge against him and not deny him the right to call an attorney. If they arrest him and he is innocent, he can bring a suit for false arrest. But this remedy is of questionable value. In most cases, the citizen who has suffered from false arrest is not able to afford to pay the expense of such a case. Nor can he find a lawyer who will take such a case. Nor is there any way to assess the amount of damages or put them in monetary terms. The remedy and the method of holding the police accountable and lessening the possibility of the misuse of police authority must be found in some way other than that of a damage suit. If the unavailability of remedy is true of suits brought against the police for false arrest and illegal search, it is even more true of instances of derogatory treatment and the use of language expressive of racial prejudice and insult and abuse.

Needless to say, the police are generally hostile to the court decisions which constitute restrictions on their law-enforcement activities. They regard the limitations on their effort to obtain evidence by "stops" and "frisks," by interrogation methods which yield confessions, as obstacles to the effective detection and prevention of crime.

They argue that to "stop and frisk" an individual often turns up evidence of crime and leads to arrests. Another argument is that the "probable cause" requirement does not apply to street detention in which the officer does not intend to make an arrest, that the police have the power to detain and question and search persons under suspicious circumstances, and that the Fourth Amendment does not prohibit this as long as the police action is within the bounds of what is reasonable use of authority and force.

A 1965 New York State statute authorized the police to stop and frisk persons when there is a reasonable suspicion that they have committed or are about to commit a crime and are believed to be armed.

The brief in support of the New York State law argued that when an officer has stopped an individual he has the right to search him if he has any reason to believe that his own safety is in danger. Thus he may "frisk" the individual, that is, pat his clothes in the search for weapons. Another more thorough frisk would be to have the suspect stand with his hands on top of a car or against a wall while the officer runs his hands from the neck down the body, under the arms, and down each leg, so that he can feel a gun or knife no matter where it is hidden on the person or in the clothing.

In most cases such a frisk might not be questioned where the officer finds a weapon or some article which is possessed or carried illegally. Generally in such instances the individual who complains about the violations of his legal rights has a very weak case. For instance, a teenager was stopped for loitering near a building where a robbery had been committed. When he was searched, a substantial quantity of narcotics was found in his pockets. He wanted to raise the question of the right of the officer to stop and frisk him. He would have had little ground to stand on, for on the face of it the officer could say he had probable cause to be suspicious and his hunch paid off.

No policy or directive should hamper the policeman in dealing with crime. But what if eight out of ten of the citizens stopped and searched are innocent? It is unthinkable and intolerable that law-abiding citizens should be at the mercy of an officer's hunches, whims, and prejudices. There will always be a gray area within which policemen differ among themselves. The study of cases might well indicate that a particular pattern is arbitrary, racially biased, and punitive. Such a study might indicate that some individual police are unduly prone to the excessive use of force or authority or language or various combinations of these.

There is also a "stop and frisk" procedure which is the result of a policy and administrative decision by the police officials in charge. The policy and practice may be characterized as that of the program of "preventive patrol" and at times as "aggressive patrol."

On this practice expert judgments are available in two sources. In his article on "Police Policy Formulation: A Proposal for Improving Police Performance," Joseph Goldstein writes:

> It is probably true that a program of *preventive patrol* does reduce the amount of crime on the street, although there has been no careful effort to measure its effectiveness. It is also apparent, however, that some of the practices included in a preventive patrol program *contribute to the antagonism toward the police felt by minority groups whose members are subjected to them.* A basic issue, never dealt with explicitly by police, is whether, even from a purely law-enforcement point of view, the gain in enforcement outweighs the cost of community alienation.[1]

[1] Joseph Goldstein, "Police Policy Formulation: A Proposal for Improving Police Performance," 65 *Mich. Law Review* 1123, 1140 (1967).

The practice is also questioned in the 1968 Report of the National Advisory Commission on Civil Disorders. In its discussion of "aggressive preventive patrol," the Report says: It utilizes

> "a roving task force" which moves into high crime districts without prior notice, and conducts intensive, often indiscriminate, street stops and searches. A number of persons who might legitimately be described as suspicious are stopped. But so also are persons whom the beat patrolman (in the local precinct) would know are respected members of the community. Such task forces are often deliberately moved from place to place, making it impossible for its members to know the people with whom they come in contact.
>
> Loss of contact between the police officer and the community he serves adversely affects law enforcement. If an officer has never met, does not know, and cannot understand the language and habits of the people in the area he patrols, he cannot do an effective police job.
>
> "Harassment" or discourtesy may not be the result of malicious or discriminatory intent of police officers. Many officers simply fail to understand the effects of their actions because of their limited knowledge of the Negro community.[2]

A number of complaints from Negroes and Puerto Ricans charge that they have been stopped, "shoved down an alley," and searched. Sometimes they are ques-

[2] "The Problem of Police Protection," *Report of the National Advisory Commission on Civil Disorders,* New York: A Bantam Book, March 1968, pp. 303–305.

tioned and searched with the purpose of establishing that they are dealing in narcotics or "numbers."

"Two men stopped my brother on the street. One forced his arm back. They searched him. One held him. They hurt his arm badly and shoved him against a car and hurt his leg bone. When they didn't find narcotics or whatever they were looking for, they identified themselves as police officers. He was visiting the United States from his home in the West Indies and he was so upset by the rough experience that he decided to leave and go back home."

A Puerto Rican teenager is carrying a suitcase for his mother. Two plain-clothes men stop him, take him into an alley, and search him. They say they find "numbers" on him. In the police station his mother says there was nothing evil in the suitcase. The boy alleges that the officers tried to plant numbers on him. He has no record.

Parents of a fifteen-year-old wrote to the police commissioner that their son was approached by a man in a Volkswagen who claimed to be a police officer and who ordered the boy into his car. The boy was afraid and refused. Two men in the car grabbed him and forced him in. He was questioned with the purpose of getting him to admit that he had dealings with a junky. He denied it. The police let him go. He was black, the officers, white.

Women who are stopped are rarely searched. When a search is made, it is usually done after arrest and in the police station by a policewoman. In one case which occasioned a complaint and a suit, a woman was forced to disrobe and submit to an intimate search in a public place. The woman in question was a member of the Spanish-speaking community. Although a policewoman searched her, the overzealous policeman's disregard of her right to privacy, to have her searched then and there in a public place, shocked his colleagues and enraged the entire ethnic community.

The abuse of authority and the violation of "due process of law" are charged frequently by minority people. They speak from many experiences in many places. Their experience begins in the South but it continues in Northern cities. For example, studies show that Negroes and other members of minority groups often undergo unnecessary and extended delay in being taken before a magistrate, that often they are not told of their right to counsel, or that they do not have to answer questions. The record shows that in Chicago many have been held incommunicado, in secret detention, 7 per cent for thirty-six hours, 15 per cent for twenty-four hours, 26 per cent for seventeen hours.[3]

In California one study[4] shows that out of 100,000 who were stopped and detained, 27,000 were released without being brought before a magistrate. Nevertheless, they were fingerprinted, photographed, and given a record without a hearing. Most of these victims were Negroes or Mexican-Americans. That members of these

[3] From a study quoted in *The Big Blue Line* by Ed Gray, Coward McCann, New York, 1967, p. 67.

[4] "Crime in California," Report of Department of Justice, State of California, 1964, pp. 49 and 111.

minority groups are dealt with without regard to their constitutional rights seems to have been of little concern to the larger community.

The Fourth Amendment provides that people shall be secure in their homes and property and persons. Search shall be made when there is reason to believe that lawlessness has occurred. There must be a warrant based upon "probable cause" and supported by an oath or affirmation in detail as to the person, place, or things to be searched and seized. Exceptions include searches made incidental to lawful arrest or in certain situations where motor vehicles are involved. But the right to search must be balanced with respect for the right of privacy, the right to be secure in one's home and person and papers. There must be no indiscriminate violation of personal privacy or invasion of homes on general "fishing expeditions."

An instance of extreme abuse of authority and of search and seizure occurred in Baltimore after the slaying of a policeman in a liquor-store holdup. For a nineteen-day period, beginning in December 1964, the police of Baltimore searched 300 homes on uninvestigated and anonymous tips, without search warrants. In these 300 "turn-ups" (investigations of a location and search of premises) four patrolmen with shotguns, submachine guns, and bullet-proof vests, invaded homes at all hours of the day and night, shining their flashlights at children in their beds, waking families. These violations were finally stopped by an injunction issued by the U.S. Court of Appeals of the Fourth Circuit.

In 1967 the searching of homes in Plainfield, New Jersey, by state police and members of the National Guard, was a classic example of the violation of the rights guaranteed in the Fourth Amendment. The police were looking for arms which had been stolen but the searches were made blindly against the Negro part of the community and were carried out without any particular reason to think that a particular home might have the stolen guns. The searchers were sadistic and indifferent to privacy and property. They left each home a shambles. More than sixty families sued the governor of New Jersey and other high state officers for the damage they suffered.

The increase in crime and the increased public awareness of the crime danger have caused people to be less concerned about protecting individual rights and more ready to grant the police the authority to ride roughshod over the right to privacy and the security against search and seizure. But the problem of lawlessness and crime cannot be solved by the police alone. And the actions of the police can make for an increase in lawlessness and violence if they act without the restraints which the people have the right to expect. To ignore basic constitutional rights and to discriminate racially in the use of authority and force are sure ways to increase the bitter rage and ruthless violence against the police and against the law and the government itself.

Over forty years ago Mr. Justice Brandeis, in his dissenting opinion in the first wire-tapping case before the Supreme Court, warned Americans against lawless law enforcement:

If the Government becomes a lawbreaker, it breeds contempt for law; it invites every man to be a law unto himself; it invites anarchy. To declare that in the administration of the criminal law, the end justifies the means—to declare that the Government may commit crimes in order to secure the conviction of a private criminal—would bring terrible retribution.

Y. D. Cases

Two cases caused the civilian members of the Review Board to question current practice in the handling of children. In one case, a police officer in plain clothes attempted to enforce the law against the sale and explosion of firecrackers around July Fourth. He thought that a small Puerto Rican girl had exploded a firecracker. He asked her whether she had. She answered no. He tried to question her further and she quite properly turned away from what to her was a strange man. When he felt that she was uncooperative and fresh he put his hand on her with the purpose of getting her into his car to take her to the police station. Other children and many of the neighborhood gathered. The child's father came down from the tenement. The officer revealed that he was a detective and that he was going to arrest the little girl. The father pleaded without avail. At the police station a "Y. D. card" was issued and the child was given a record at the precinct house and at the Youth Division Headquarters of the Police Department. Investigation showed that it was not absolutely certain that this child had set off the firecracker. Many had been set off by many children. The child had not been in any trouble, and, on the contrary, had a good record at school and in the neighborhood. For a little girl to have such a police record in the view of the Puerto Rican community was a serious disgrace. The members of the Review Board referred the case for conciliation. It was understood that an effort would be made to explain the assignment of the police and the importance of preventing the accidents which occur inevitably when children play with firecrackers. The conciliation officer reported at a later date that the officer was willing to go along with having the record expunged if that could be arranged with the Youth Division. The father and family of the child were in much distress and felt that the damage to their daughter and the family was so great that they might return to Puerto Rico unless the record could be expunged.

The second case involved the actions of an off-duty policeman. He was relaxing on a bench in the park near his home. Children were running and jumping over the benches and he was annoyed. He asked them to play elsewhere. After they ignored his request, he became angry and was alleged to have grabbed a little Negro girl and to have shaken her and thrown her against a bench. The child's mother came up in a fury. The officer then revealed that he was a policeman and he proceeded to give the child a Y. D. card. The Review Board agreed that this case should be conciliated and that the Y. D. card should be expunged if possible. Investigation revealed that the officer had been exceedingly troubled by the incident and was quite ready to remedy whatever harm had been done. The mother of the child was ready to conciliate the matter. She was afraid the incident might result in her eviction from an apartment in a middle-income project.

Because of these cases, members of the Review Board, two civilians, and one police member visited the Youth Division and had an opportunity to learn the history and purposes and methods of this division of the Police Department. It was made clear that the issuance of a Y. D. card is at the discretion of the officer and that it is not strictly an arrest but a "contact." Nor does the child have to answer "Yes" if he is ever asked whether he has been arrested. The card is confidential to private and most public agencies. Exceptions are employment or appointment in the Police Department itself and also in National Security positions such as the C.I.A.; in the Peace Corps, etc. Finally, it was made clear that there was no means of expunging the Y. D. card from Police Department records. Apparently a technical difficulty exists in clearing the I.B.M. tape in Central Records and a greater difficulty lies in the City Charter regulation that the approval of the Board of Estimate of the city is required to destroy any city record. One serious disappointment was the failure of the Police Department to expunge the record of the Y. D. cards in the two cases referred to. As a result of this, the cases could not be conciliated even though civilians and police were quite ready in each case to cooperate in a constructive reconciliation. The illogical bureaucratic result is that both cases were classified as "unsubstantiated." But in each case there was little dispute of the facts and there was readiness of the police to admit that some wrong might have been committed. Here, then, is an anomaly which should be corrected. It has to do both with off-duty police conduct and with the Y. D. card itself, its issuance, its meaning, and the conditions under which it can be expunged to remedy injustice.

Special Groups

The job of the police is especially difficult in handling certain special classes of individuals, namely alcoholics and narcotics addicts, vagrants and derelicts, prostitutes and homosexuals, and the varieties of non-conformist youth. These groups present behavior problems which are complicated by recent liberalizations of the law and by changing and ambivalent attitudes toward the morality of behaviors which traditionally have been considered immoral if not criminal.

There is a tendency to assume that such persons need not be respected and that their constitutional rights need not be protected. Most of the persons who fall under these classifications hesitate to make civilian complaints. But those that do are often indicative of a far larger number of violations which are never reported.

If an individual has an epileptic seizure or if a spastic walks and acts abnormally, there is no violation of the law or the moral code of the community. If police do anything it must be to help and protect the individual. If an individual is emotionally disturbed and mentally ill, his actions may be disturbing to others and the community, but here again the action called for today is that of protection and aid. It was not so many decades ago that societies, thinking such individuals possessed by evil spirits and bewitched, had them beaten, put in stocks, or held up to public ridicule.

An alcoholic may be destroying himself. He may be disturbing to the community. But today an enlightened community believes that if he is addicted to alcohol or to narcotics, he should be treated as a sick person and not as lawless unless he breaks the law. According to Justice Abe Fortas:

> a state may not constitutionally inflict punishment for an illness, whether the illness be narcotics addiction or "the common cold." . . . We are told that some 6,000,000 Americans are afflicted with alcoholism and that each year more than 1,500,000 arrests—three of every eight—are for drunkenness.

Punishment may be no deterrent.

Not many years ago it was common practice for the police to round up the drunks. Drunkenness was considered a crime and alcoholics were arrested and convicted and sent away.

The tendency today is not to consider drunkenness as such a crime. New York's revised Penal Law, which became effective on September 1, 1967, declares that "A person is guilty of public intoxication when he appears in a public place under the influence of alcohol, narcotics, or other drug *to the degree that he may endanger himself or other persons or property or annoy persons in his vicinity*. Public intoxication is a violation." (Emphasis supplied.) This makes it clear that a man can no longer be arrested merely because he is drunk, but only if he is disorderly, disturbs the peace, threatens people, etc., in a public place.[1]

This is not to say that all the police in every part of the city leave the drunks alone. Those who constitute the "men on the Bowery" are often the victims of rough handling, even when they are not violating city ordinances or being technically a nuisance. When public feeling about their condition or their behavior causes embarrassment, or when guilt and irritation reach a certain level, the police may revert to discarded policies of long ago—especially in the poorer parts of the city.

There are some who say that the alcoholic poor were better off when the policy was one of dragnet and arrest, that the alcoholic actually benefited by being brought in. He was forced to take a bath or shower, to have his clothes deloused. He was given a good meal, and received treatment which would "dry him out," as well as a medical examination which might reveal illnesses such as tuberculosis, diabetes, or others which might be treated.

Even though the Police Department may have ceased its mass arrests, and the courts have stopped sentencing those who have committed no criminal act but have been found in a state of intoxication, the question still remains, How does the police force treat alcoholics? At the time the Review Board was functioning, many complaints alleged mistreatment and some alleged brutality.

[1] This law had been adopted in 1965, but was not yet effective during the period of the Civilian Complaint Review Board operation.

Most of them were unable to produce witnesses or evidence to substantiate their allegations.

One resource now available is a special agency, "Operation Bowery," for the care and treatment of alcoholics. Specially trained workers are available. Police officers may assist in moving individuals if they are present or are called.

Another group are persons whose behavior has brought forth not only condemnation but also extreme neglect from even the most moralistic elements in the community—the idlers, vagrants, beggars. These are the men without jobs, homes, or families. They are the migratory men—the drifters and the refugees from their own pasts. These are the men who move in and out of the "Skid Rows" of the nation, the inhabitants of the flophouses and the missions. To many in the larger community they are an eyesore and an embarrassment, at times a nuisance and even a menace. They approach cars at red lights. They spill out into the upper-class sections of the city in rags, begging for a cup of coffee just when people in their best clothes are about to enter an expensive restaurant or the theater or opera. They are especially disturbing to the clergy and the politicians whose public image must be that of compassion and concern for all human beings.

It has been police practice to round up these men even when they have not violated the laws of society, civil or criminal. Their violation is that they exist. They represent their own failures and the failures of society to deal with their problems. The handling of a tramp or hobo or bum on Skid Row is no pleasure. But each is a human being and a citizen. His plight may not be entirely of his own making. If the police act rough with these outcasts it is also evidence of the calloused conscience of the community.

In the case of prostitutes, the traditional method was to organize a vice squad of plain-clothes men who walked the streets and arrested those who solicited, or followed the couple and broke in on them. Subsequently, it became police practice to stage periodic mass arrests of prostitutes in the streets of the city, even without evidence of an act of prostitution or the specific act of soliciting. Thousands were picked up on charges of "disorderly conduct," and held in jail overnight. After Legal Aid Society lawyers defending the women charged illegal arrest, the Police Department on advice from the district attorney made arrests on the charge of "loitering."[2]

Do the police enforce the law by dealing with the act of soliciting or do they go beyond this? Prostitution exists. Prostitutes are held in contempt and many assume that they have no rights—sometimes that they are fair game for a lucrative "take." There are many who know the collection points at which police are paid protection money for leaving the prostitutes and brothels alone.

In matters of sex, the police are often the enforcers of traditional morality. This is particularly true in the case of the homosexual. In the past, homosexuality, even when

[2] According to the new Penal Code effective September 1, 1967, a person is guilty of prostitution only if there is a specific offer to "engage in sexual conduct with another person in return for a fee."

practiced by consenting adults, was considered evil, sinful, and aroused the extremes of repugnance and outrage.

But today public attitudes are changing. More homosexuality is found among educated and upper-class people of both sexes, and there is increasing acceptance of sexual behavior as a personal and private affair so long as it does not make a nuisance of itself in public places—and so long as it is not coerced. It is more often viewed as the product of some abnormality in the emotional structure of the individual outside the realm of criminal charges and punishment. There is growing awareness that the homosexual, too, has his rights in due process of law, and in the protection of his life, liberty, property, and pursuit of happiness.

But the homosexual still suffers harassment and exploitation by the police. Plain-clothes men have been staked out for the express purpose of being solicited. The officer may ask a likely youth for a cigarette light. He strikes it rich when the youth says, "I can give you more pleasure than a thousand girls."

The police have kept certain restaurants and bars and hangouts under surveillance, and made arrests there. A typical complaint originating in the effort of police to deal with homosexuals is illustrated in the following case: Police in plain clothes go to a tavern reputed to be a hangout for homosexuals. The complaint read as follows: "A stranger told my friend and me that we were under arrest. I asked him what for and he said Section 106 of the A.B.C. Law. I informed him that I was a patron of the premises and that the arrest was illegal. He demanded that I stand in the middle of the lounge and used obscene language. I remained seated at the bar and finished my drink. He spoke to me in an abusive manner and ordered a patrolman of the ——— Precinct to bring us to the station house for arraignment. I told him I wanted to call my attorney. He refused to allow me to make the call. I would not go willingly, as the arrest was unlawful. Two days later, in the Criminal Court of New York City, the judge dismissed the charge. I charge the police officer with abuse of authority and false arrest and the use of derogatory language. (In the comment on the back of the complaint form the C.C.R.B. investigator wrote "Complainant apparently in possession of all his faculties.")

Derogatory Treatment

People hurt one another in many ways. When the police violate the feelings of people, it is especially bad because there is no recourse. The bruising of the ego and the violation of dignity and respect are increased in this kind of one-sided confrontation. The victim is powerless. An officer may stop a man and detain and question him and do it slowly, so as to delay and irritate and bait him so that he may finally say or do something which will justify police action. This is harassment. If the police stop a car and ask everyone to get out and identify himself, and then address the driver with, "What are you doing in this town, Charlie?" or search the car for small violations —these make for the deep resentment and rage which can never be entirely healed. So, too, phrases in an arrogant tone and voices used with a generous sprinkling of four-letter words, obscenities, and threats make for hatred toward the police.

There is a brutality of physical force and a brutality of words. And there is a brutality of attitude and gesture. A man can stand and look and glare with contempt. An officer can show it by the way he enters a home or makes a search. "Derogatory" is the allegation made more frequently in complaints than any other—except "physical brutality."

The use of derogatory language, the attitudes of arrogance and contempt may even be more serious than the excessive use of force or authority. For the minority community suffers not merely from material poverty and discriminatory treatment, but, even more, from the feeling of lack of respect. Self-esteem is seriously damaged when people are told every day by word or attitude or treatment that they are not so good as their fellow humans. No people can stand this unless they have tremendous inner strength and psychological and spiritual supports which can sustain their belief in themselves. When the entire impact of the dominant majority community is callous to their needs and their suffering and their grievances, and when, in addition, they are humiliated and rejected, the effect is disastrous to mental health.

Here are a few examples:

A young man was looking frantically for his mother. She was senile and had wandered away from home. He approached a police car and asked for help. He was sure she had wandered about in the neighborhood streets. The police officers paid no attention to him. He repeated his appeal for help. One of the officers told him to "drop dead!" and drove off.

A Puerto Rican couple had gone to the police station for help about their daughter. The girl was fifteen years old, emotionally disturbed, and was now living with and being exploited by a man of forty. The priest had advised them to go to the police station and have the girl committed. They came in during the early evening. Neither of them spoke very good English but they made it quite clear to the sergeant at the desk that their daughter was in trouble and that they wanted to get her to therapy or an institution. He laughed at them and said, "The only way to deal with your daughter is to shoot her." Then he kept them waiting for about an hour and a half and did nothing to help them. The mother wept. Finally the captain of the precinct came in and asked what these two people were doing sitting there. At that point the couple were able to explain their predicament to the captain.

Another complaint reads:

"This police officer has contempt written all over his face. He seems to hate young men who aren't in uniform. He stands at the corner and sometimes out in the middle of the street and stares and glares and seems to assume that we are all homosexuals or what he would call 'draft dodgers.' He's so full of hate. Couldn't he be moved to a different beat or precinct where there aren't so many students?"

On a hot summer afternoon a public swimming pool was overcrowded. Police were called to keep the crowds in order. They moved forward with arms locked. An elderly man was in the way and could not move fast enough. He fell and his leg was injured. The officer nearest to him said, "Good!"

Another complaint reads:

"He abused me verbally. He called me names. I'm against calling people names like 'nigger' and 'spic.' But what did the patrolman say to me? I'm a thirty-four-year-old man, law-abiding, have studied at six colleges, and am a veteran of the Korean War, and he calls me, 'Hey, kid.' He wouldn't dare talk to a *black* man like that! But I'm white. I won't tolerate being talked to that way by police."

Another complaint:

"I'm sitting in my car, and an officer asks me, 'Is that your car?' I say, 'Do I have to answer that question?' The officer says, 'Do you want a bloody head?' Then he demands my registration. Then he demands identification. I produce my driver's license. Then he threw my registration and license and summons on the street and drove away."

"We had a quarrel in my home and we were noisy. Someone called the police. The officer came and acted annoyed at having to come and he used abusive talk. I had to tell him to leave my house."

"I had some trouble with my kids and I called the police. One of the police used profane and dirty words and called my daughter a prostitute and a street walker and bragged that he has a gun and can use it any time. Then he said—he don't give a damn what I do because he will retire soon anyway."

A bystander witnesses what he believes is brutality against a helpless victim who has done nothing which threatens the police. He approaches and asks a question. An officer speaks, "Who the hell do you think you are, a policeman? Mind your own business or we'll take you in, too."

A police officer pulls up alongside a driver who stops for a red light. "Get the hell over there!" he yells. Then when the driver stands at the curb alongside of his car the police officer yells, "God damn it, who the hell do you think you are going in such a f——in' hurry?" He spews hostility and personal exasperation.

The driver says, "Listen, Officer, I was obeying the law. I'm a careful driver. You can give me a summons or arrest me but don't talk to me like that. I'm a citizen and a taxpayer. Just because you wear a uniform and have police authority is no reason to talk to a citizen this way. Give me a summons or arrest me or leave me alone. Cut out the obscenities and abuse. I don't have to take it from you. Now what's it going to be?" The officer turns and gets in his car and drives away.

One form of derogatory treatment shows itself in attitudes toward mixed racial couples. Again and again couples of two different racial backgrounds are stopped and asked to identify themselves. This is a form of discrimination and of insult and humiliation. It is generally assumed that they are not married and that the woman is a prostitute. Many examples of such harassment and violation of personal freedom and right of privacy take place on Skid Row and the more Bohemian centers such as Greenwich Village.

One example of a complaint on this matter was the case of the police officer who walked near and alongside of a mixed couple, a white man and a Negro woman. He spat in front of them. He did this repeatedly. The couple took his shield number and made a complaint. The officer denied that he had prejudice and that he was expressing contempt and hostility. He said he had a catarrhal condition and that he had to spit. Should a police officer who cannot accept the existence of mixed couples be assigned for duty in a modern cosmopolitan urban center?

Racial and Ethnic Slurs

In the depression years unemployment hit the Negro community first, and harder than the white. In some blocks as many as 80 per cent of the employables were laid off. Some husky Negro workers tried to get work on the docks. On their way back from work on the docks at the lower end of the city they were waylaid by a white gang and beaten with lead pipe. They ran.

The head worker of a neighborhood settlement heard their feet as they raced to escape. He heard the cries of those who were caught. He telephoned for police: "Officer, it looks like a race riot! We need help!" When the police arrived, the social worker brought out some of the Negroes who had sought shelter in the settlement. Instead of asking for a description of those who had been guilty of assault and disturbing the peace and disorderly conduct, and instead of going out to find the lawbreakers, the police sergeant said, "Why don't you niggers stay up in Harlem where you belong?" These were the exact words used to James Baldwin when he was ten years old and walked in streets outside the ghetto. He was frisked and left flat on his back in a lot. Millions of the souls of black people have been seared in childhood just this way.

The individual demands respect. It is humiliating for a man to be the helpless victim of derogatory name calling, names which mean devaluation of the individual and the minority group, often accompanied by words which are insulting and expressive of prejudice.

Many complaints allege the derogatory language of racial and ethnic prejudice:

"After I identified myself, the officer made indecent statements about Negroes. I told him he should not stereotype black people as thugs or call us niggers. He said, 'All you niggers are troublemakers,' and he stressed the Watts riots, Chicago, Harlem, Bedford-Stuyvesant. After about fifteen minutes, some police patrol cars drove up and a few of the officers told him to leave me alone, that I am not one of those smart busters. He left, and three officers who seemed to sympathize with my position stayed and consoled me. Where police are so unreasonable and bitter, I fear what they may do to any Negro."

A Negro police officer is alleged to have said to a white person under arrest, "I hate all white people."

An Italian complains that a policeman issuing a summons answered the protesting motorist with "You Guineas are all alike!"

A Negro driver makes a right turn and a police car has to jam on its brakes. "You dumb nigger bastard!" calls the policeman.

A Negro graduate student objects to being stopped and questioned. "You niggers are troublemakers!" says the officer.

"I work in the community center. I work with the kids. Some of the teenagers were fooling around with the man who owns the delivery truck for the drugstore. So the drugstore man must have thought the kids were going to rob him and he phones the police. The kids start to walk away when the police come. That's when one of the police calls out, 'Come here, you black niggers.' But the boys kept walking and the police left."

> Physical abuse is only one source of aggravation in the ghetto. In nearly every city surveyed the Commission heard complaints of harassment of interracial couples, dispersal of street gatherings, and the stopping of Negroes on foot or in cars without obvious basis. These, together with contemptuous and degrading verbal abuse, have great impact in the ghetto. As one Commission witness said, these strip the Negro of the one thing that he may have left—his dignity, "the question of being a man." [1]

In the past, people accepted the attitude and language of their devaluation. But times have changed. If the police wish to be respected, they must give respect. If the police wish trust and support in their difficult and dangerous work, there must be a change in the way they speak to their fellow citizens.

When children play and fight, they say, "Sticks and stones can break my bones but words can never hurt me." But the words of a parent or teacher can be destroying words if they reject or devalue the person. And the

[1] "Police Conduct," *Report of the National Advisory Commission on Civil Disorders,* New York: A Bantam Book, March 1968, p. 303.

words of the police are strong words. They have the badge of authority behind them to back them. They have the power to intimidate. And when they are said with contempt, they humiliate. When they are said with curses or obscenities, they are insulting and degrading. When they are said with weapons, a club, a gun, or handcuffs and the authority to arrest, then they are powerful words, and then they are one-sided words, unanswerable words that silence, words that destroy the self—or they are words that enrage and lead to hate and violence. For words can make men want to hurt and fight and kill.

Demonstrations

A demonstration is not a crime. Neither is it a riot. But the mishandling of a demonstration can lead to crime and riot.

The National Advisory Commission on Civil Disorders quotes the FBI riot manual for law-enforcement officers as follows:

> A peaceful or lawful demonstration should not be looked upon with disapproval by a police agency; rather, it should be considered as a safety valve possibly serving to prevent a riot. The police agency should not countenance violations of law. However, a police agency does not have the right to deny the demonstrator his constitutional rights.[1]

Demonstrations are legitimate methods of expression by groups of citizens who hold that their rights are violated or that public policy is counter to their deepest concerns—especially when their beliefs are intense and the ordinary methods of persuasion and education and the ballot are denied. Demonstrations are legitimate if carried out with respect for the rights of those who dis-

[1] *Report of the National Advisory Commission on Civil Disorders,* New York: A Bantam Book, March 1968, p. 323.

agree and if they do not endanger the community or obstruct its essential functions. Demonstrations are a form of freedom of expression of democratic process and basic constitutional rights.

But for the police, demonstrations present difficult problems. Some demonstrations are planned and carried out in an orderly constitutional manner within the framework of legality. If, however, these actions are based on cynical disillusion with democratic procedures and with the purpose of disrupting the community and creating chaos, then the issue is far more serious. It is not always easy for citizens or officials or police to know the real intent and motivation.

Citizens may use the method of non-violence. They may lie down or go limp. How deal with them without brutality and without violating basic rights? If they obstruct the traffic or essential community functions, the police may have to use force to remove them and restore legitimate community channels of mobility.

It is important not only that protest be protected but also that the rights of others and the community be secured also. It is important that the police be held accountable for what they do. At no point should they make their own prejudices police and public policy.

If the protesters abuse the police with offensive language and taunts and provocation, should the police, nevertheless, act with some restraint? If they use violence and throw stones and bottles and use weapons, should the police respond with force? Violence may break out because of the excessive action and overreaction of the police. The victims may cry "brutality." A wise and sophisticated community will know what is involved and will wish to provide for some objective review of the facts of the case.

Non-violent demonstrations and marches do not always remain non-violent. The flare-up of physical conflict and the destruction of property and injury and death may occur because the demonstrators or marchers are not firmly under a united discipline or the control and clear directives of their leaders. Violence may break out because of the attacks of opposing groups or hostile audiences or rival groups with opposing ideologies.

Thus a demonstration and parade and sit-down may generate counter-demonstrations of groups with extreme and violent intentions. How shall this be dealt with justly?

One such case which came to the Review Board is a good illustration of this problem: In 1966 a militant Negro civil-rights leader was leading a delegation to press for the restoration of funds for youth programs in the ghettos of the city. The group's method was to wait on the steps of City Hall in order to confront the Mayor. By chance the same day there was a demonstration by landlords and homeowners. One delegation was composed predominantly of Negro youth and the other group was predominantly adult white. Both were waiting on opposite ends of the steps of City Hall. Some of the landlord delegation thought they recognized the militant civil-rights leader. They shouted and struck at members of the Negro delegation with their picket signs.

The police set up a barrier to keep the two groups apart and to make sure that the Mayor would have a way through when he arrived. But at a certain point some of the Negro group, aroused by the name calling, wanted to go through. The Negro leader asked them to take a vote. Either as a result of the vote or because the group couldn't be controlled, some moved across the barrier. The leader and a woman from his group locked their arms around each other, so that it would be difficult to move them. The police had to tear them apart, and in doing so one of the police was kicked. The police grabbed the leader and carried him into City Hall by his feet and his arms. He charged "brutality," stating in the formal complaint that he and the woman with whom he had locked arms were beaten by the police who were "racially motivated." The bitterness of the occasion was due partly to the race issue, partly to the property issue. It seemed to the Negro group that they, and not the whites, were made to move.

The police report held that "The testimony of disinterested witnesses substantiates the police version that to prevent a widespread disorder at City Hall the police cleared the steps. . . . The police use of force in effecting these arrests was necessary and proper."

Still pictures and television movie films were shown a number of times to try to get as clear a picture as possible of what happened. The decision was to hold a hearing. But before the hearing took place, the Review Board was terminated. (It is precisely in such situations that a free press and mass media, by this objective reporting, bring an invaluable service to the larger cause of freedom and justice.)

The case is given in some detail in order to illustrate the difficulty in getting facts and making a judgment as to what is proper police performance and what is in the category of "brutality" or "unnecessary use of force." The case is typical. It raises many of the problems inherent in demonstration cases.

In the first place, such cases are bound to be accompanied by strong emotions and high tensions on all sides. Intergroup conflicts may add to the volatile atmosphere. This makes it especially difficult to get a true picture of what actually happened.

Second, where there is mass activity and large numbers of police move rapidly in and out of the crowd, it is hard to get accurate identifications of particular policemen who are the subject of complaints. In addition, if many are in plain clothes, it is not easy for demonstrators to know which actions are done by police and which by civilians.

Third, the larger the number of participants and the larger the number of witnesses after the action is over the more varied the stories. The many accounts are likely to be so contradictory that they elicit as much doubt as they do trustworthy evidence. Only if a person is able to participate and maintain a keen objective observation and clear memory can his testimony give effective support to allegations. Most civilians are not trained to bring together the detailed facts so that they can prove that what they allege to have happened did actually take place.

Finally, it is possible that the very characteristics of the civilian complaint review board which give it strength—its objectivity, and impartial investigation and reviews may be just the qualities which may have little appeal to the leaders of demonstrations and protest movements. For the most part, militant and extremist leaders do not want a quiet, confidential, judicial hearing. They want a dramatic and widely publicized clash which will catch the attention of the people and win their support. Those who stress reason and non-violent demonstrations, parades, meetings, picketing, and sit-ins, may want support and protection for orderly protests. But on every major social issue there are those who actually welcome brutality by police. It is "front page" and on the top newscasts when police drag demonstrators by their arms or heels on the street pavement, use night sticks on the heads of non-violent persons, and make random arrests of persons who happen by or who, by their non-conformist dress, make the police think that they are among the "troublemakers." Such actions by the police are regarded as excellent publicity for the demonstrators' cause. They help overcome public apathy. They make people think. They win sympathy. And they make the members of the "movement" more angry and united.

One important factor in peace demonstrations is that the police—perhaps to a higher percentage than the general population—are likely to have strong nationalistic and militaristic feelings favoring any war in which the United States is involved. They tend to have some prejudices against pacifists and conscientious objectors and all war protesters. Proper enforcement of their double task of protecting the expression of peaceful protest and of protecting demonstrators against possible violence by counter-demonstrators becomes especially difficult.

The problem of dealing with anti-war groups was well illustrated in New York City in the week of December 5, 1967. Demonstrations were designed to close down the induction center at Whitehall Street in lower Manhattan and to gain as much publicity as possible for the protest movement against the war in Vietnam. The public read about the demonstrations in the press, heard about them on radio, and had opportunity to view police actions firsthand on TV. Among the many accounts of how the demonstrations were handled, the following quotes indicate how the *New York Civil Liberties Union Bulletin* of January 1968 interpreted police action:

> Since the protest had been planned for some time, and was no secret, the police were massed and ready for the worst. The streets and sidewalks surrounding the induction center were blocked off swiftly and professionally so that the demonstrators were forced to assemble in two large groups several blocks removed on either side of the center.
>
> But the disobedience was entirely symbolic: Spock and his followers were led single file through a maze of barricades, allowed to sit down for a few seconds on the sidewalk in front of the steps, and then were ushered just as peaceably into the paddy wagon, which departed to the scattered cheers of the assemblage.
>
> This almost liturgical protest continued for most

of the day until over 250 protesters had been obligingly arrested by the police. Almost all were charged with disorderly conduct, despite the fact that their conduct could not have been more orderly. . . .

Many demonstrators threatened to do far worse on Wednesday and Thursday, and everyone believed them. Expecting widespread violence, the police arrived on Wednesday with an even greater show of force. Now there were several thousand police; soon they would easily outnumber the demonstrators.

But very little of the expected violence materialized: no marbles thrown under police horse's hoofs; no ammonia squirted; no bottles thrown; no lead pipes. Undoubtedly there were some demonstrators who did commit acts which were indefensible and for which they should have been arrested. But by and large the large-scale fear of violent protest proved unfounded. . . .

On the first day, while there were incidents of police misconduct (one ACLU staff member had his rib cracked by a night stick), for the most part the police acted with restraint. By Thursday, however, that restraint had evaporated. . . .

On Thursday, and also on Friday, many people who were arrested were manhandled, hit with night sticks, charged at by horses, and in general treated quite roughly. Much of the most serious violence was perpetrated by plain-clothes men who were identifiable only by small colored buttons (green on Thursday, orange on Friday) which they wore on their lapels. Since they did not wear badges with numbers, they could not be made accountable for their behavior. It was quite clear that the police wanted to avoid accountability. On several occasions police were seen to go into a rage whenever they observed anyone taking down their badge numbers. On one occasion several policemen attacked a New York *Post* reporter who was taking notes, beat him, and tore up his notebook. By this behavior, and by having hundreds of unidentifiable plain-clothes men on duty when there was obviously no need for undercover work, the Police Department avoided accountability and encouraged abuse. . . .

On Thursday, near the United Nations, scores of peaceful picketers were arrested on the orders of one police inspector after having just been told that they could picket by a different police inspector. They were arrested, told they were being charged with parading without a permit, taken to the police station, held for a few hours, and then released. Later the police said it was all "an honest mistake." Yet by Friday that explanation seemed dubious at best because the same thing happened near Bryant Park. In any case, whether or not a demonstration is legal is not a matter for police discretion; it is a matter of law. Walking on the sidewalk (which is all the demonstrators were doing at both the U. N. and Bryant Park), even while carrying posters and chanting slogans, does not require a permit, and is not illegal in and of itself. It is beyond the police power to decide whether or not demonstrators should be allowed peaceably to assemble. That is a matter of law, and the law clearly permits it. In fact, the purpose seems to have been illegally to break up the demonstrators: by Friday afternoon, the police had completely lost their ability to distinguish between disorderly conduct and free assembly.

> And yet the police regulations issued to all police by Chief Inspector Garelik prior to the week of December 4 were a model code of police behavior. The police were specifically instructed to protect and not interfere with peaceful demonstrators; to use night sticks only defensively; not to wade into a crowd en masse when in pursuit of one person in that crowd; and to use stretchers to carry off demonstrators who went limp instead of dragging them along the street by the hair. All these instructions were both given to and ignored by substantial numbers of police. The plain fact was that there was anarchy, confusion, and conflict in the Police Department: captains were seen arguing with patrolmen; inspectors gave contradictory orders, regulations were flouted. . . .

When the police use clubs and other weapons on demonstrators, there is always the question whether the force they used was necessary. Under experienced and competent police officers, demonstrators can be assured freedom of expression and kept within bounds consistent with community order. But if the police in their zeal or in their hostility toward demonstrators and protest groups lose restraint and permit their prejudices to direct their actions, the result is likely to be violence. Where hostile counter-demonstration groups are determined to resort to violence against anti-war groups, the police shirk their responsibility if they turn their backs when hostile citizens attack the demonstrators.

Police interference with the distribution of anti-war leaflets resulted in a number of complaints to the Review Board. At demonstrations and on a number of other occasions police had stated that permits were needed or else charged a violation of the anti-littering law. It was the police members of the Review Board who were the first to point out that no permit was required and that non-commercial literature dealing with issues of social and political concern could be distributed freely. Indeed, instruction to police trainees on such questions had been part of the program at the Police Academy.

The distribution of leaflets is an expression of freedom of speech and the press guaranteed under the first Amendment of the Constitution. Training courses in the Police Academy make it clear that leaflets on social and political issues are permitted whereas commercial leaflets are not. According to the New York Civil Liberties Union, which has filed many cases against what it terms a widespread pattern of harassment of leafleters, the actions of the police hamper the exercise of free speech. In many instances the mere threat of a summons or arrest is enough to discourage the exercise of constitutional rights. Here some police have acted out of their own prejudices, or under the pressure of citizens to make the police express their social and political attitudes. Thus according to one complaint the officer in charge of a police patrol prevented leaflet distribution on the insistence of an off-duty policeman who felt strongly about the issue involved. In another case the complainants were handing out anti-war leaflets outside City Hall. When they refused to identify themselves they were charged with littering and given a summons.

The extreme forms of such police action are the cases

where fanatics beat up a speaker and break up a meeting. The police sometimes turn away while this occurs. And when the violence is over, the police move in—not to arrest those who were guilty of assault and of disturbing the peace, but to arrest and manhandle the beaten speaker and those who dare to protest.

In early struggles of workers to organize unions and to win the right to collective bargaining, the police sometimes charged into the striking pickets without playing the impartial role of keeping the peace between employers and employees. In the depression years many union meetings and meetings of the unemployed were broken up and the leaders arrested and beaten—some fatally —by the police.

Although the practices of police have changed in most labor-management disputes, in the anti-war demonstrations and the anti-Vietnam protests the public witnessed police actions and sometimes the failure of the police to protect the demonstrators against the savage attacks of their opponents. In December 1967 the police turned their backs when the longshoremen beat and stomped the anti-war demonstrators. It was not the dockworkers who were restrained from using their muscle and longshoremen's hooks by police commands or the threats of police clubs:

". . . there was a brief clash when a group of husky longshoremen attacked some demonstrators.

"The police arrested several protesters after breaking up the clash with the dockworkers near the Staten Island

Ferry terminal. None of the longshoremen was arrested. . . ." [2]

At the AFL–CIO conference in Miami, Florida, the head of the International Longshoremen's Association boasted of the longshoremen's behavior and the fact that the New York City police had not seen fit to charge anyone with assault.

Abuse of authority is involved in the complaint of illegal search and arrest of individuals in a picket line before the arrival of the President of the United States for a speech at the Waldorf-Astoria Hotel. One complainant stated that her bag was searched, that she was detained and ordered to answer questions and denied the right to a lawyer, and that words such as "filthy Communist trash" were used. The case was brought to criminal court in July 1966. The charges were then withdrawn when the assistant district attorney moved to dismiss the case:

"The People are prepared at this time to move to dismiss the charges against the defendant on the ground that the evidence is insufficient to establish her guilt beyond a reasonable doubt. I understand that she is prepared to stipulate to hold harmless the police officer, the city of New York, from any civil liability. . . ." The case was dismissed. (An example of the way a complaint or possible damage suit for false arrest can be gotten rid of by the police with the cooperation of the district attorney and the judge.)

A number of complaints which came to the Review Board alleged that police had stopped young men of

[2] *The New York Times,* Friday, December 8, 1967.

draft age and had asked them to identify themselves by showing their draft cards. Police members of the Review Board were the first to be critical of this practice. It is not a responsibility of the New York police to enforce the Selective Service Act or to enforce the requirement that young men of draft age should carry their draft cards. If the police want to check identification, the draft card is not the best way to do it. It has no home address. This kind of demand for identification is a form of harassment to those of fighting age who are not in the military service. Such police practice might well be interpreted to be an example of the policeman's prejudice toward pacifists, conscientious objectors, or toward young men who may be deviant in dress or appearance. The Review Board developed the policy and practice on more than one such complaint of referring the case with recommendation of "instructions" for the police officer. Not only was the officer instructed that this was not appropriate conduct on his part but also the problem was called to the attention of those responsible for training at the Police Academy.

An important decision by the U.S. Court of Appeals for the Second Circuit recently laid down guidelines for the police and for officials in charge of parks and such places as the bus terminal of the Port of New York Authority. The court ruled that the Port Authority Bus Terminal was an appropriate public place for peaceful political expression.

> The admission of charity solicitors, glee clubs, and automobile exhibitions without untoward incident

> evidences the ease with which the Terminal accommodates different forms of communication. . . . Provocative and controversial the discussion may be, but in the excitement generated by political controversy our preconceptions and prejudices are tested. The framers of the Constitution opted for the disharmony of controversy because they believed that in that unrest lay the best prospect of an ordered society. . . . We believe the Port Authority may not abridge [the] right to choose this place any more than they can control [the] choice of message. We hold that the Constitution precludes the Port Authority from enforcing a plenary prohibition of speech within the Terminal. (The ruling held that the anti-war protesters could stand with placards, distribute leaflets, set up tables with literature, and that they should be protected by the police in their constitutional rights. The action was begun in 1966. Decision was handed down in 1968.)

In high-voltage emotional situations such as demonstrations, the police face difficulties requiring strategy and restraint. They have four responsibilities: to permit the demonstration, to protect it from hostile forces, to protect the community, and to protect themselves. Clear directives should come from headquarters. Police should be present in adequate numbers. They should not include the young untrained or the undisciplined. Only veteran police, experienced and carefully selected, trained, and under the supervision of officers experienced in handling demonstrations, can assure maximum protection of freedom of expression while maintaining social order.

Fortunately, most people have a humanity which sometimes enables them to reach beyond their prejudices. There are a simple decency and a saving sense of humor which often correct our fanaticisms. Even in the midst of the tensions between citizens and police at an anti-war demonstration, basic humanity of human beings sometimes comes through. At the Whitehall anti-war demonstrations, between the period of non-violent quiet and the later period when things got out of hand, one policeman was seen to be showing the pictures of his children to Dr. Benjamin Spock. For a moment he saw Spock, not as the fanatical pacifist and treasonous enemy, but as the pediatrician and human being who all his life had worked to save children's lives. So also the anti-Vietnam demonstrator saw the cop as a civilian, the father of children, and a man.

At the second demonstration before the Waldorf-Astoria a policeman and a boy confronted each other for the second time:

"Hi, Officer!" said the boy.

"Hi, Mickey!" said the officer. "How you doin'?"

"I'm doin' all right. Thanks," said Mickey.

"How you doin' in school, Mickey?"

"I'm doin' better. Officer, don't you be too hard on us today."

"Don't *you* be too hard on us, Mickey," said the officer.

Why Was the Civilian Complaint Review Board Defeated?

Even before the Board was appointed, the Patrolmen's Benevolent Association had drawn up a petition to force a referendum in the form of an amendment to the City Charter on the issue of having civilians on the Review Board. The validity of the referendum was upheld by the Court of Appeals, and it appeared on the ballot on November 8, 1966, worded as follows:

> "PETITION"
>
> FOR THE SUBMISSION TO THE ELECTORS OF THE CITY OF NEW YORK OF A LOCAL LAW TO AMEND THE NEW YORK CITY CHARTER, TO REQUIRE THAT ALL MEMBERS OF ANY REVIEW BOARD ESTABLISHED TO INVESTIGATE AND PROCESS CIVILIAN COMPLAINTS AGAINST POLICEMEN BE FULL-TIME MEMBERS OF THE POLICE DEPARTMENT, THEREBY PROHIBITING ESTABLISHMENT OF A REVIEW BOARD COMPRISED IN WHOLE OR PART OF CIVILIAN MEMBERS. . . .

The Patrolmen's Benevolent Association mounted an effective campaign with expert public relations and large financial support of between $500,000 and $1 million drawn from families and friends, from police organizations in many parts of the country, from conservative groups, and from those who saw the Review Board as a threat to their values. The extensive propaganda campaign stressed arguments appealing to the fears and prejudices of many sectors of the population:

1. It was stressed by those in charge of the campaign that the Review Board with civilian participation would tie the hands of the police in fighting crime. Press advertisements and TV commercials pictured the police with their hands tied or handcuffed while a white girl walked down a dark street in a setting which suggested that she might be assaulted at any moment.

2. It was pointed out that the Review Board was demoralizing to the police. A policeman was pictured as saying, "Next time I turn my back!"—implying that the way to avoid civilian complaint was by inaction. It was also stated that police would resign or retire, thus leaving the Police Department undermanned and the people unprotected.

3. It was argued that the Review Board was an interference with the authority of the police commissioner and that it would be impossible for the Police Department to control its own discipline.

4. It was stressed that civilians are unqualified to judge police performance and that civilians were likely to be biased against the police. Only the police are in a position to understand the police problem and review civilian complaints.

5. It was charged that the creation of a Review

> Board with civilian members represented political interference with police operations and showed the danger of leaving the Police Department at the mercy of politics.

The campaign against the Review Board took place at a time when many of the people were reacting to the increase in crime and the riots which had taken place in a number of cities. The personal fears of the people, the white backlash against the Civil Rights Movement and the thrust of "Black Power" were part of an atmosphere in which the anti-Review Board campaign was particularly effective.

Among the groups campaigning against the Review Board were the Patrolman's Benevolent Association, the Fraternal Order of Police, the Conservative party, the American Nazi party, the Renaissance party, the Birch Society, the Brooklyn *Tablet,* and the *Daily News.*

Sometimes the campaign raised critical issues concerning which men of good will might differ. But much of the campaign was on a lower level and appealed to prejudice, attempting to undermine public confidence in the integrity of the Review Board itself. It was suggested by some extremists that the Review Board with civilian participation was part of a Communist plot to undermine police organization and to bring about the breakdown of law enforcement.

An editorial in the August 18, 1966, issue of America's *Reporter* for the combined textile industries published in Greenville, South Carolina, was headed "License to Riot." "Did you see the pictures of those

Cleveland riots, of Negro thieves running wild, in and out of wrecked establishments, arms loaded? And did you see the cops standing by, idly watching the debauchery? That was the result of a Police Review Board."

In the increasing tension and excitement of the referendum campaign some police officers used their authority to restrain advocates of the Review Board who distributed literature, leaflets, campaign buttons, and posters. People were arrested on charges of "disorderly conduct" and "littering." In one case a man who was pro-Review Board and distributing leaflets was made to move and was then arrested while the individual distributing anti-Review Board material across the street was unmolested. In another case a minister was charged with "peddling without a license." The Police Department Legal Affairs Bureau joined with the American Civil Liberties Union in getting this case dismissed. When a young couple protested the carrying of an anti-Review Board sticker on a police patrol car, they were arrested for disorderly conduct and fined.

Analysis of the referendum vote reveals that the Irish, German, and Italian sections of the city voted heavily against the Review Board. The Review Board won a majority in one borough, Manhattan, owing to the Negro and Puerto Rican vote and the liberal white vote. But in most of the city (See Appendix: Results of Referendum Vote) Negroes and Puerto Ricans did not vote at all on this issue. Since those who live in the ghettos suffer most from crime, many may have been more concerned about police protection than fearful of police brutality.

Some may have been confused by the "Yes" and "No" issue as it was put to them. But the bulk of the city, white and middle class, was conscious of insecurity in the streets and probably reacted out of fear and prejudice concerning the Negro. Some of the voting may have represented partisan politics on the part of those against the Republican administration in a usually Democratic stronghold. Certainly all those who were enmeshed in the corruption and graft involving the police may well have feared that the involvement of civilians in the Review Board might at some point be a threat to their interests.

Many groups had special reason for their attitudes. Cabdrivers, for example, have traditionally been antagonistic toward the police. In the past a typical comment would have been, "They're bastards. They take it out on us. They give us a ticket and bring us to court or the Hack Bureau for no reason at all. We never get a square deal. I'm suspended. No work or pay for three days—just like that! You can even lose your license for good."

But in 1966 almost all of the taxi drivers were against the Civilian Complaint Review Board. They felt the need for protection more than the need to fight the police. Why had they changed? They thought they were exposed to more danger from the Negro and other minority groups than from the police. Many resented a Negro passenger. It meant no tip or a poor one. It meant having to drive to Harlem or Bedford-Stuyvesant or some other minority and poverty area with no return fare. It meant fear of a knife at the back of the neck and the loss of a day's earnings in a stickup—hopefully without injury.

Usually they were sure it was a "colored guy." It might be someone who had come up from poverty and had "made" it. Now he was living high and taking it out on other people for what he had suffered—discrimination and deprivation.

There are over twenty-two thousand cabdrivers in New York City. They reflect the prejudices of the people generally. One with a European education says, "I'm a refugee from Hitler's racism. I survived and here I am driving a cab. A Negro gets in. Sure he has reasons to gripe. But he doesn't know what I've been through. He doesn't know I'm a victim of racism, too. Sure I know what the Negro has suffered in America. But what does this man do? He rides me. He takes his unhappiness out on me. 'You aren't driving straight,' he says. 'You're going the long way.' I say, 'This is the shortest way I know. If you know a better way, tell me. Be my guide!' Then he says I'm going too slow. I say, 'Watch the speedometer and see! I can't break the law.' Then he uses obscenities. Finally I've had enough. I pull over. I stop the car. I say, 'If you don't like my driving get another cab. I don't need to take your guff! I don't need your fare!' So he quiets down. I wish I could've taped it. If he had brought me up to the Hack Bureau on charges they'd have backed me. Anyway, that's why I voted against the Civilian Complaint Review Board. It hurt me to do it. I should know better with what I've been through—especially with Nazi police brutality."

Although top-level political leaders of both major parties came out for the Review Board and lent their names in the campaign, they had little effect. Many thought the Review Board was a decent and civilized approach to some of the difficult problems in the relation of police and the people, but that they did not believe it was "realistic" in the political climate and social tensions of the time.

A vote YES *for* the Amendment meant the abolition of civilian participation in the Review Board. To retain the Review Board required a vote of NO. Doubtless many voted YES thinking they were supporting the Board and many voted NO thinking they were abolishing it. The chances are that the confused wording worked in favor of those who wanted to abolish it.

Besides the Amendment requiring that only policemen could serve on the Review Board there was a "sleeper" clause which abolished civilians on the supervisory staff. It read as follows:

> Neither the Mayor, the Commissioner, nor any other administrator or officer of the City of New York shall have power to authorize any person, agency, board or group to receive, to investigate, to hear, or to require or recommend action upon, civilian complaints against members of the Police Department except as provided in this section.
>
> Attendance by police officers. No member of the Police Department or other person shall be disciplined or otherwise penalized for his failure to appear before or respond to the inquiries of any person, agency, board, or group appointed by the Mayor, the Commissioner, or any other administrator or officer of the City of New York to receive, to investigate, to hear or to require or rec-

> ommend action upon civilian complaints against members of the Police Department unless such person, agency, board, or group shall be duly appointed in accordance with the provisions of this section.

Most of the voters had no clear understanding of the meaning of the Amendment. Even those who voted YES and meant to abolish civilian participation in the Review Board did not know that there was a provision in the Amendment that would make it impossible for civilians to work in the top supervisory staff as well as on the Board. The executive director, the conciliation officer, and the two hearing officers would have to be chosen from personnel who had worked for the Police Department for at least a year. For example, the two hearing officers who had been selected because of their education, legal training, and their experience in conducting hearings could be replaced only by men working regularly in the Police Department. Henceforth the Civilian Complaint Review Board would be a police operation from top to bottom: investigations, conciliations, hearings, and review.

An Appraisal: Problems and Strengths

The short duration of the Review Board precluded the opportunity to learn from experience and to devise ways of improving the effectiveness of its operation. The members of the Board were responsible for civilian complaints made after June 30, 1966. But they were not appointed until July 11. The review of cases, which doubled after the establishment of the Board, had to await the recruitment and appointment of the four civilian members of the supervisory staff: the executive director, deputy director, and conciliation officer, and two hearing officers, who were not appointed until late July and early August. As a result, the number of cases under investigation, and not quite ready for review, tended to accumulate. When the Board was terminated on November 8, almost half of the cases were still under investigation or in process of being conciliated or were involved in hearings.

The widespread lack of information and the intense emotional controversy over the Board made it easy for people, both those for and those against the Board, to spread and to believe misinformation and distortion.

Apart from the discussion and argument which took place concerning the Board during the referendum campaign, most people and most of the police knew very little about the way the Board functioned. The requirement that the members of the Board preserve their judicial character meant that they could not participate in the campaign even to the extent of speaking to the public or the police about how the Board was organized or how it actually functioned.

An educational program to inform civilians about the Board's areas of jurisdiction and where and how to make known their complaints, would have given confidence to many groups of the population,—especially the very poor and the members of minority groups, who had the least knowledge that they had rights and that their rights could be considered by an impartial agency. Moreover, those who made complaints had no awareness of how important it was to identify the police by precinct and shield number or how to substantiate their allegations with witnesses and objective evidence.

There were civilians who believed that the Review Board staff could not be depended upon to do a real investigative job because they were all employees of the Police Department. Actually, the civilian supervisory staff had the kind of education and experience which fitted them admirably for the work. They had to be persuaded to leave good positions in law and government to join the Civilian Complaint Review Board. No group could have had more devotion and competence. The complaint supervisor, Inspector Arthur Savitt, and Deputy Inspector Jerome Stolk brought high standards and integrity to the work. The rank and file of the staff were experienced and trained and identified with the agency.

The Review Board brought about a fairer climate for dealing with civilian complainants. In the past, and in many police review boards today, the complainant would be surrounded by police personnel. In contrast, the presence of civilians on the executive staff and on the Review Board gave a sense of security and fair play. This made a great deal of difference to those civilians of low income and those lacking in education or unfamiliar with the English language, all of whom had always been at a disadvantage in interrogation, hearings, and cross-examination.

A ground-breaking development which had been provided for in the General Order No. 14 was tested and worked well. This was the provision for conciliation. Whereas formerly as many as 92 per cent of the complaints had been thrown out as unsubstantiated, now it was possible to adjust many grievances where there was evidence of some police error or rudeness or where there was misunderstanding, ignorance, or false expectation on the part of a civilian.

For the complainant this procedure presented the Police Department as an agency which was ready to consider civilian feelings and rights. The individual received attention. He might be informed and educated as to his mistaken expectations or his understanding of the law and the responsibilities of police. Many civilians have no knowledge of the special priorities of some police assignments. Most civilians have no knowledge at all of the regulations which govern police action. In addition, the complainant had some assurance that the officer complained against was aware that civilians could be heard from and that police were accountable for their behavior and the use of their authority.

An educational program among the police might have made the work of the Board easier and more effective. Most of the police were convinced that the Board was biased against them. Actually, this was far from the fact. One of the valuable and lasting accomplishments of the Review Board was the development of a Bill of Rights for the police. Those officers against whom there was a complaint were assured that they could know the allegations against them, that they would have an attorney and the right to a fair and impartial hearing, where they could have the allegations explored in a non-accusatory and a non-punitive atmosphere, where they would be safeguarded in all legal rights.

If allegations were found to be unsubstantiated, the officer would receive a letter to that effect and there would be no notation of the complaint in his career folder. If a complaint was made while he was being considered for promotion, the investigation would be expedited so that, should the complaint be cleared, there would be no obstacle to his promotion.

The two key elements in investigations would be an honest quest for the truth and impartiality. The best evidence that these factors were at work was to be found in the reactions of the attorneys who worked on the regulations and who represented the police in hearings. They were well satisfied that the procedures and operations were fair.

The conciliation program was of value because it could confront an officer with the fact of neglect or a mistake or misconduct and help him correct his ways without leaving a blemish on his career record in the Department. (Previously, every complaint went into his record.) If the effect of the error was not serious enough for recommending charges to the police commissioner, the Review Board worked out an in-between form of dealing with the problem. This meant an "instruction" from the officer's immediate superior in the precinct or division, or a discussion with the complaint supervisor or conciliation officer of the Review Board.

Most of the police thought that the Board diminished the powers of the police commissioner, and represented political interference with the operations of the Police Department. But under General Order No. 14, the police commissioner continued the policy of the past which was that the decisions of the Board were only advisory. They were an aid to the police commissioner in making his decisions. They in no way diminished his authority or his controls of the disciplines of the Police Department.

Indeed, the flow of complaints to and recommendations from such a board constitute an invaluable feedback for the police commissioner, affording him day-to-day knowledge of the grievances of the people in various parts of the city, the knowledge of popular reaction to police practices and police behavior, and a surer knowledge of how well the Police Department is doing its job.

The police commissioner acted on the recommendations according to his own discretion. In a number of cases the disciplinary action taken by the police commissioner might well be judged to be slight and ineffective. Instead of dismissal, a reprimand or a suspension, a shift in assignments, or demotion to a lower rank, might be appropriate. The problem from a larger social viewpoint was not to punish anybody but to make sure that the misconduct would not be repeated by the particular officer or by the rank and file of the Police Department as a whole. If an officer had given evidence of extreme and chronic misconduct or signs that he could not learn or change, then for his sake and the welfare of the Police Department and the public he should find other work.

As for the Review Board itself, if the civilian members had felt at any time that the processing or investigation of complaints was inadequate, or that their findings and recommendations to the commissioner were being ignored or poorly used, they could easily have reported and discussed their criticisms with the commissioner or could have resigned with a public statement giving the reasons why. This was in no sense a "kept Board."

At no time in the four months were the Review Board members split into police and civilian factions. In almost two hundred complaint cases investigated and brought to the Board for review, there were only two cases on which, after discussion, there was a split vote in the final decision. The rest of the decisions were unanimous. In both these cases a police officer and a civilian paired to make the final vote two to five. Respect and trust and good will increased steadily throughout the four months of the Review Board's operation. On all matters there was a maximum of objectivity, an atmosphere of problem solving and a minimum of emotional or personal controversy. The seven Review Board members had been strangers to one another. They became friends. Although they worked together for only four months and did so in the midst of a stormy political controversy over their agency and functions, they worked quietly, confidently, and with high morale.

A distinctive contribution of the Review Board was mutual education. The police members educated the civilians on police problems, regulations, policies, and standards, and the civilians brought their own experience and viewpoint to the work from a number of fields of human relations with a fresh outlook unconditioned by the traditions of or identifications with the police. This made it possible for all the Review Board members to bring a broader and deeper understanding to many of the cases under consideration.

The civilians had to learn the working definitions of "stop and frisk," arrest and arraignment, disorderly conduct, etc. The police members were sources of information concerning the handling of guns, regulations governing the search of motor vehicles, and the laws of leafleting and littering. In turn, the civilians questioned practices concerning the arrest of children and the issuance of Y. D. cards and police records, the policy concerning off-duty policemen. They recommended more specialized training for police in Puerto Rican neighborhoods, especially the study of the language and customs and culture of the people. They raised questions about the ways in which police asked young men for identification, the attitude toward mixed interracial couples, and the rights of homosexuals and prostitutes, alcoholics and derelicts, police conduct in demonstrations and intergroup conflicts.

Had the Board been in existence earlier and for a longer period than four months, the civilian members would have learned more through orientation and contact with the men of the force. It might have led to a greater status and competence for the entire Civilian Complaint Review Board as an agency. Doubtless there would have been a higher percentage of cases from the very situations which were responsible for the gap between the people and the police.

No one would claim that the Review Board as it was established in New York City in 1966 was a panacea. It could not solve the tough problems which people and police had to face. But it could and did contribute constructively in the way it dealt with complaints and it may have contributed to easing tension and building confidence that the relationship between the people and the police would be more cooperative than it had been. It is impossible to establish a measurable cause-and-effect relationship to prove that the Review Board made the difference between a city at peace and a city with riot and violence. But the suffering and irritation owing to excessive heat and the water shortage of 1966, added to other tensions, might well have brought extreme strife if something hadn't been done. That something was the strategy and discipline of the Police Department, a serious effort to improve police-community relations, and the tireless efforts of the Mayor and his administration. But the Review Board may have helped. It did its work quietly and confidently. Its members remained out of the controversy over its existence. While it existed there were doubtless many who kept their hope and faith that the relationships of individuals and groups in the city might overcome the fears and hates which separated them.

That the Review Board included police and civilians, that it included Negro and Puerto Rican, and that it was an interfaith group, gave it a representative character. It included civilians who represented diverse elements in the community and a concern for the people in the low-income and racial ghettos as well as for the mass of middle-class citizens. The Board was tough in its standards of police performance and its exacting demands on complainants. But it was balanced, just, and humane.

It is with this background that the recommendations of the National Advisory Commission on Civil Disorders should be studied, especially the section of the report relating to "The Problem of Grievance Mechanisms":

> In the context of civil disorder, appearances and reality are of almost equal importance in the handling of citizen complaints against the police. It is not enough that there are adequate machinery and procedures for handling complaints; it is also nec-

essary that citizens believe these procedures are adequate. Some citizens will never trust an agency against which they have a grievance. Some irresponsible citizens will attempt to provoke distrust of every agency. Hence some police administrators have been tempted to throw up their hands and do nothing on the ground that whatever they do will be misunderstood. These sentiments may be understandable, but the police should appreciate that Negro citizens also want to throw up their hands. For they believe that the "police stick together," that they will cover up for each other, that no officer ever receives more than token punishment for misconduct, and that even such expensive legal steps as false arrest or civil damage suits are foredoomed because "it is the officer's word against mine."

We believe that an internal review board in which the police department itself receives and acts on complaints—regardless of its efficiency and fairness, can rarely generate the necessary community confidence, or protect the police against unfounded charges. We also believe, as did the Crime Commission, that police should not be the only municipal agency subject to outside scrutiny and review.

Incompetence and mistreatment by any public servant should be equally subject to review by an independent agency.[4]

[4] "The Problem of Grievance Mechanisms," *Report of the National Advisory Commission on Civil Disorders*, New York: A Bantam Book, March 1968, pp. 310–311.

Conclusion

What people do to people is not just a police problem. It is a community responsibility. If there is police brutality, it should be recognized that there is also civilian brutality.

One of the problems of the police is to protect people from hurting and injuring each other. And one of the civilian problems is how much brutality by civilians, and by police, the public is willing to tolerate, for civilians tend to turn away and to condone brutality when it is exercised upon other persons. Those who want security and protection at any price too often close their eyes and do not want to know what the police do. This tendency gives tacit approval to brutality and the violation of basic rights. It makes the police agents of the deadened conscience of the community. It means that civilians as citizens become party to any methods, no matter how illegal and how unconstitutional and how immoral, just so they can feel more secure.

Democratic society requires both freedom and order. If freedom is excessive, the result is license and anarchy. If lawlessness is excessive, there follows the cry for more police and strong-arm methods. The excess of repressive methods in the use of police authority and force makes for extreme anti-governmental rebellion and anti-police hostility.

Democratic process brings with it a certain amount of disorder compared with a totalitarian and dictatorship system. Human beings can stand only a certain amount of disorder and confusion and violence. Human beings cannot value and use freedom unless they have a minimum of security. If personal anxiety goes beyond a certain limit, the individual begins to overvalue security and order and law and force. He may call for more police and more authority and armament for the police. He assumes that these will not be used against himself but used against other people, against his neighbors. But when he does this he is laying the basis for abdicating his freedom and yielding to a small group the power to regiment and coerce the people.

Crime is not just a police problem. The mounting crime rate is not due to police inadequacy. Crime is the result of inadequate family life, poor schools, evil forces in local neighborhood life, and the distortions of human personality by poverty and racial discrimination and violations of basic human needs. Police are only one factor in what must be a multipronged program for crime control and crime prevention.

Riots are not just a police problem. The riots of recent years and those which are almost inevitable in the years immediately ahead are due to the same factors which make for crime. But to these must be added at least the following characteristics: first, riots are not like the acts of individual criminals or organized-crime syndicates.

The riot involves a substantial part of a community, a mass, spontaneous action much like a flash fire. Second, riots are highly emotional expressions of hatred against the people who embody or symbolize the power structure or ruling power system. Third, riots are essentially destructive: to burn down or blow up the society which imprisons, deprives, and stifles human beings.

When they face crime, riot, and militant protest movements the police feel that they are in a war situation. Certainly their obligations in these situations are not in the same class as helping an old lady across the street. But even when they face the ruthless brutality of the criminal killer or the bitter violence of the riot or the planned and stubborn pressure of demonstrators, the police have to act as a disciplined professional group. The way a police force deals with each and the extent to which it maintains a strategy and a discipline and a competence can make all the difference between effective democracy or a police state.

When a democratic community elects officials to administer the government of a city, the citizens should obey their officials and the laws and they should support the enforcement of the laws. But they should also make certain that the public authority they have delegated and entrusted to their officials is used within the framework of the Constitution and with proper regard for the basic human rights of every citizen. The people as well as their mayor and his commissioners are responsible for the use of public authority.

This is why the way police carry out their duties cannot be left to them alone. When the citizens delegate legal authority and give weapons to the police, they must retain final control and demand accountability for the way authority and force are used.

The provision of persons and agencies to receive the complaints and grievances of the people is one of the ways in which a democratic community can ease tension between the people and their officials. The concept of a review agency is applicable to the uses of authority by all public officials and functionaries.

Today the increased role of government in the common life and the increased part played by government functionaries in decisions which affect the citizens and the community have made it more necessary than ever that the citizen have some recourse to agencies which will give him a hearing when he believes that he has been the victim of the abuse of authority by government agencies or their personnel.

This need is especially great in the urban situation because the size and interdependence of the city make men dependent upon one another and upon city government for essential services. Citizens depend upon many kinds of public officials and employees such as teachers, welfare workers, housing officials, building inspectors, tax collectors, and the police. There are many possibilities for abuse of authority, arbitrary decisions and personal bias. Incompetence, neglect, and dishonesty in services of vital concern to the people have to be dealt with effectively and impartially. The complaint review agencies—the idea of an outside and an inside audit—constitute a development which is necessary, desirable and inevitable in a just and democratic society.

Appendix

I Biographic Material on Civilian and Police Members of the Review Board

II Volume of Complaints

III Ethnic Origin of Complainants

IV Nature of Allegation in Complaints

V Results of Referendum Vote (*New York Post,* November 9, 1966)

I. Biographic Material on Civilian and Police Members of the C.C.R.B., July 1 to November 8, 1966

Mayor Lindsay named four civilian members to the seven-man Review Board. Police Commissioner Leary named three members of the Police Department to serve on the Review Board.

ALGERNON DAVID BLACK, CHAIRMAN OF THE BOARD

Algernon David Black was born in New York City, November 18, 1900. He attended public school and the Ethical Culture Schools, and was graduated from Harvard College with a B.A. in 1923, magna cum laude, and Phi Beta Kappa.

He joined the staff of the New York Society for Ethical Culture in 1923 and was elected a religious Leader in 1934. He is a member of the Fraternity of Leaders of the American Ethical Union.

He served on the staff of Hudson Guild Settlement in 1923–1924 and as Headworker of Madison House Settlement 1926–1930.

He was a founder in 1946 of the Encampment for Citizenship and served as Educational Director for fifteen years.

He was Co-Chairman of the City-Wide Citizens' Committee on Harlem from 1941 to 1947; Chairman of the

New York State Committee Against Discrimination in Housing 1948–1963, Chairman of the National Board of Directors of the National Committee Against Discrimination in Housing from 1950 to 1967.

He is a member of the Board of Directors of The American Civil Liberties Union and the Citizens' Committee for Children.

During and after World War II he acted as voluntary arbitrator on Labor-Management Cases with the American Arbitration Association.

He has worked as teacher, social worker, arbitrator, radio commentator, and as a religious leader.

MANUEL DIAZ

Manuel Diaz was graduated from City College of New York in 1951 with a bachelor's degree in sociology. He obtained a master's degree from Columbia University School of Social Work, writing his thesis on "The Attitudes of Puerto Ricans in New York City to Various Aspects of Their Environment."

Since 1950 he has worked with a number of social action programs. He was Assistant Chief of Group Work and Community Development for Mobilization for Youth, Inc., 1962–1964, and director of Community Affairs and Special Projects for MFY, 1964–1965.

He took his present post with the Puerto Rican Community Development Project, of 143 West 72nd Street, June 1, 1965.

He has served as an instructor at three colleges, as an

advisor to the New York City Youth Board and on Group Work, and Recreation Committee of the Community Council of Greater New York.

He served on a number of civic associations including the Police-Community Relations Committee of the Monroe County (New York) Human Rights Commission, the East Harlem Council for Community Planning, and the Puerto Rican Family Institute.

DR. WALTER I. MURRAY

Dr. Walter I. Murray received his B.S. in mathematics and social science from Indiana State College in 1937, his M.S. in education from Indiana University in 1944, and his Ph.D. in education from the University of Chicago in 1947.

He has been a Professor of Methods of Teaching at Brooklyn College for the past ten years.

He is an expert in the anti-poverty area, is the author of several articles dealing with the problems of the poor, and is coauthor of the book *Educating the Culturally Disadvantaged Child,* published this year by David McKay Co., Inc.

Dr. Murray has served as educational consultant to groups in New York City; the Westminster-Watts area of Los Angeles; Hackensack, New Jersey; Norfolk, Virginia; and Sodus, New York.

He served on the Board of Directors of the NAACP and the Urban League in Phoenix, Arizona, and wrote a tentative manual for the Phoenix Police Department entitled, *The Law and Human Relations.*

THOMAS R. FARRELL

Thomas R. Farrell, received an A.B. in economics from Colgate University in 1949 and an LL.B. from Columbia Law School in 1952.

He has been admitted to practice before the New York Appellate Division, Second Department; the U.S. Supreme Court; the U.S. Court of Appeals for the Second Circuit, and U.S. District Courts for the Southern and Eastern Districts of New York.

He is a member of the Association of the Bar of the City of New York and has served on its Committee on Municipal Affairs since 1963. He was one of the draftsmen of a report prepared by that Committee which recommended in 1965 the creation of a Civilian Complaint Review Board.

He has been a member of the Bronx Chapter of the Catholic Interracial Council since 1963 and served as its President, 1964–1965. He successfully urged the Chapter to support creation of a Civilian Review Board and campaigned actively in speaking engagements and letters to newspapers for its creation.

EDWARD J. McCABE

Edward J. McCabe has been the Police Department's deputy commissioner in charge of the division of licenses since September 9, 1960.

Commissioner McCabe came to the Police Department after more than twenty-five years of service with the Federal Bureau of Investigation.

During this quarter century of federal law-enforcement work, he participated in the investigation of hundreds of important cases including the acid blinding of newspaper columnist Victor Reisel, the Brinks holdup in Boston, and the Weinberger kidnaping on Long Island.

At the time of his retirement from the FBI, he was agent in charge of the FBI office in New Haven, Connecticut. Earlier, he had been second-in-command of the FBI office in New York and had served in San Francisco, Detroit, Boston, and Washington.

Commissioner McCabe, a native of the Bronx, graduated from St. Regis High School, received a B.A. degree from Fordham College, and got his LL.B. degree from Fordham University Law School. He was admitted to the practice of law in New York State in 1933.

Before joining the FBI, Commissioner McCabe was a volunteer civil and criminal trial lawyer with the Legal Aid Society of New York.

PEARSE P. MEAGHER

Pearse P. Meagher is a deputy inspector currently assigned as administrative officer of the Fifth Division, which encompasses Manhattan's upper West Side.

Inspector Meagher has been a member of the Police Force since June 9, 1941. He was promoted to detective in 1946, to sergeant in 1948, to lieutenant in 1951, to captain in 1957, and to deputy inspector on May 2, 1966.

While he was captain, he commanded the 23rd Precinct, the 41st Precinct, and the 44th Precinct.

Inspector Meagher holds two departmental citations.

Born in the Bronx, Inspector Meagher was educated at St. Regis High School, got a B.A. at St. Peter's College, Jersey City, an M.S. at Fordham University, and a LL.B. at Fordham Law School. He has completed all course work toward a Ph.D. in public law and government at Columbia University.

During World War II he served in the Navy. During the Korean War he held the rank of captain in the U.S. Air Force.

Inspector Meagher has been active in a wide range of community endeavors and has received numerous community awards. He has also participated in many Police Department administrative functions, serving as a member of the Police Department Charity Committee, assistant chairman of the Board of Trustees of the Police Pension Fund, chairman of the Superior Officers Council, the collective bargaining agent for all officers above the rank of patrolman, and president of the Lieutenants' Benevolent Association.

He was recently admitted to membership in the American Academy of Political and Social Science.

FRANKLIN A. THOMAS

Franklin A. Thomas, has been the Police Department's deputy commissioner in charge of legal matters since

October 25, 1965. As the department's chief legal officer, Thomas serves as legal adviser to Police Commissioner Howard R. Leary, supervises the department's legal bureau consisting of 30 attorneys, and directs the department's legislative program.

Before joining the Police Department, Thomas was an assistant United States Attorney for the Southern District of New York, an attorney-adviser in the office of the Regional Counsel of the U.S. Housing and Home Finance Agency, and a legal assistant in the office of the general counsel of the New York State Insurance Department.

Commissioner Thomas graduated from Franklin K. Lane High School in Brooklyn and got his B.A. at Columbia College, where he was captain of the varsity basketball team and was cited as the most valuable player in the Ivy League in 1955 and 1956.

Following his graduation from college, he served four years in the U.S. Air Force. He now holds the rank of captain in the Air Force Reserve.

After discharge from the Air Force, Commissioner Thomas entered Columbia Law School, from which he graduated in 1963 with moot court honors. He is a member of Phi Delta Phi Legal Fraternity and a director of the Columbia Law School Alumni Association.

II. Volume of Complaints

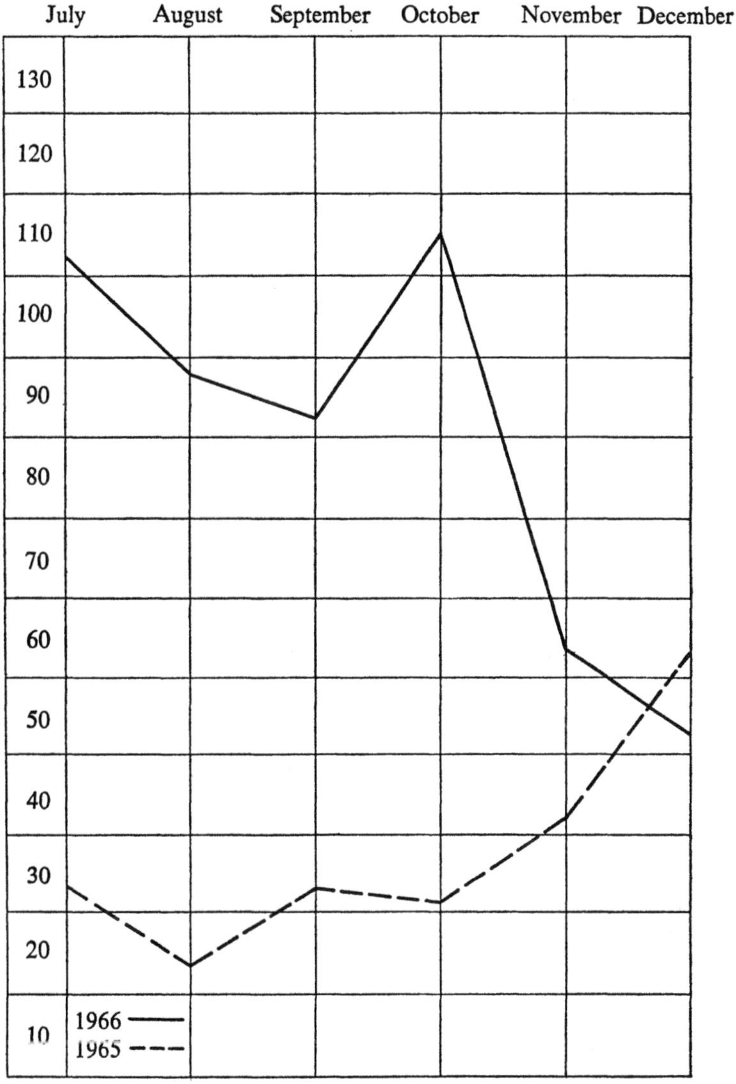

Volume of Complaints

July 1/66 to December 31/66 in comparison to July 1/65 to December 31/65

III. Ethnic Origin of Complainants

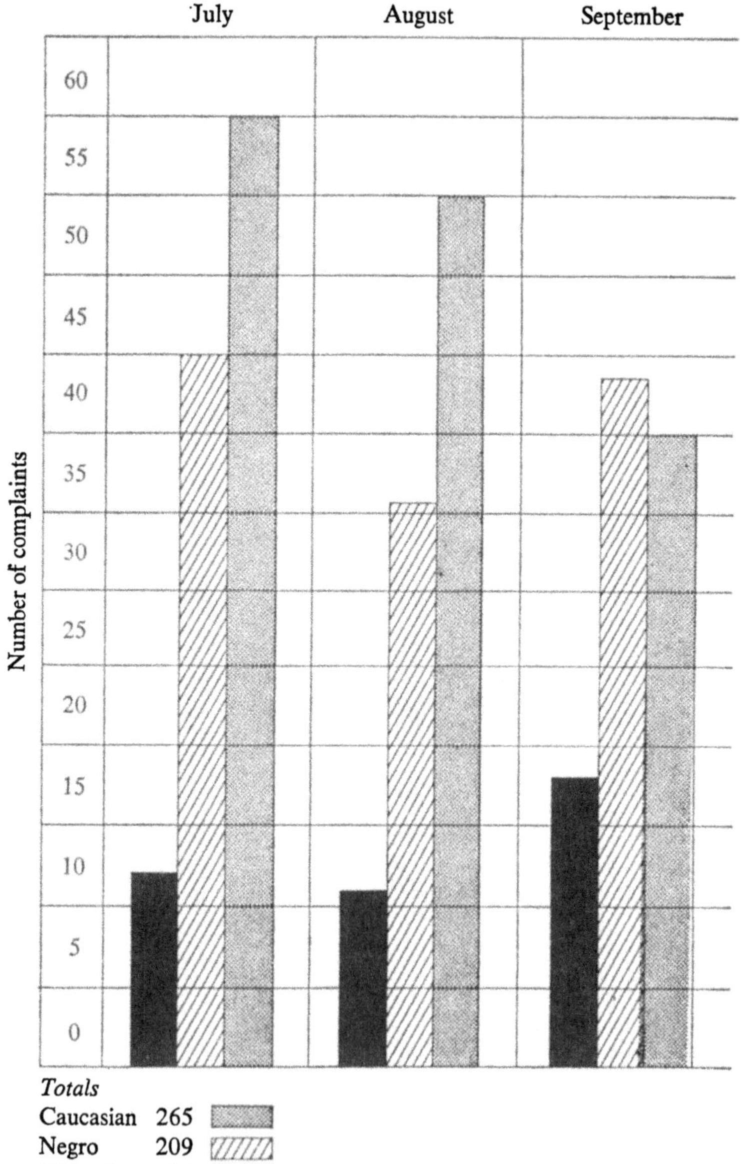

July 1, 1966, through December 31, 1966

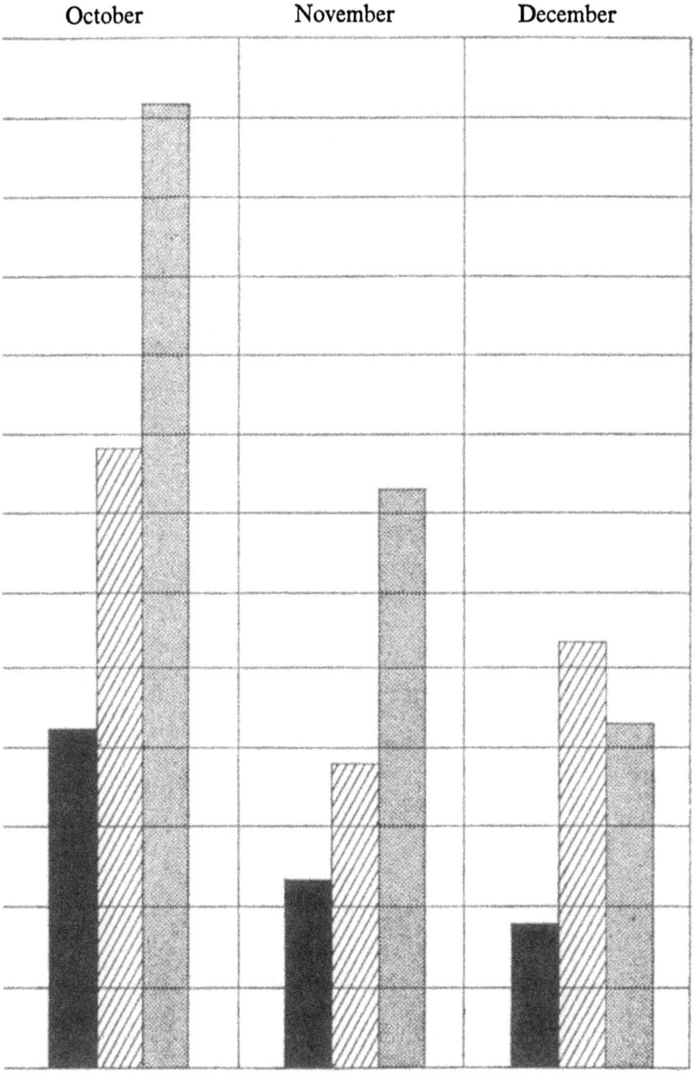

IV. Nature of Allegation in Complaints

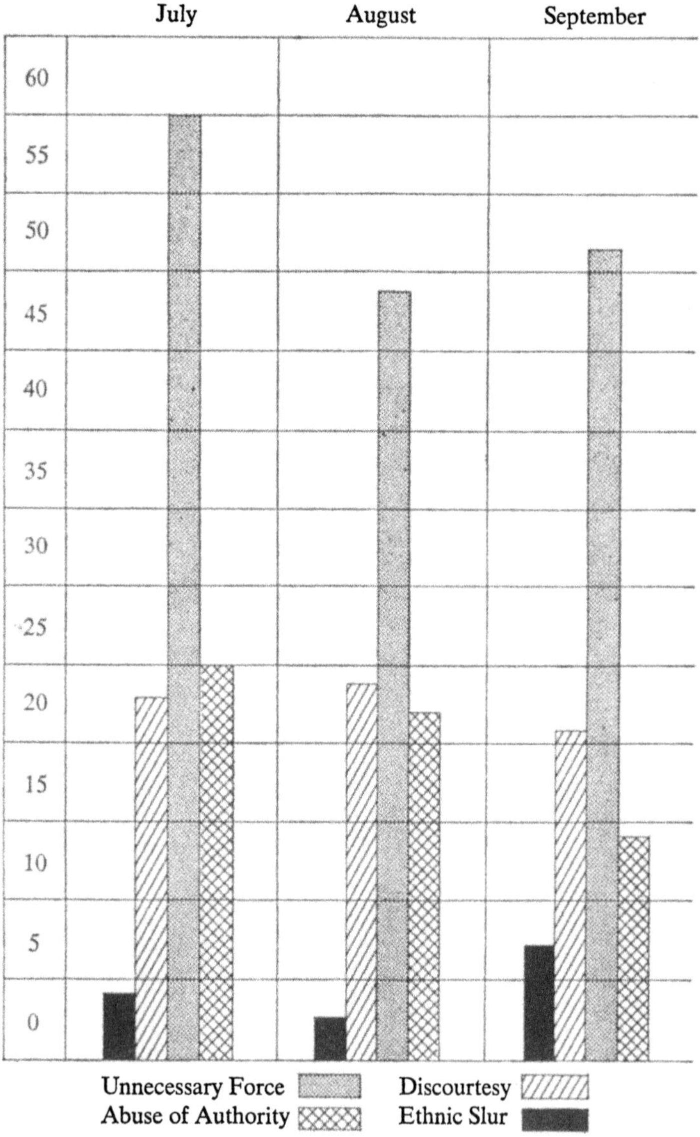

July 1, 1966, through December 31, 1966

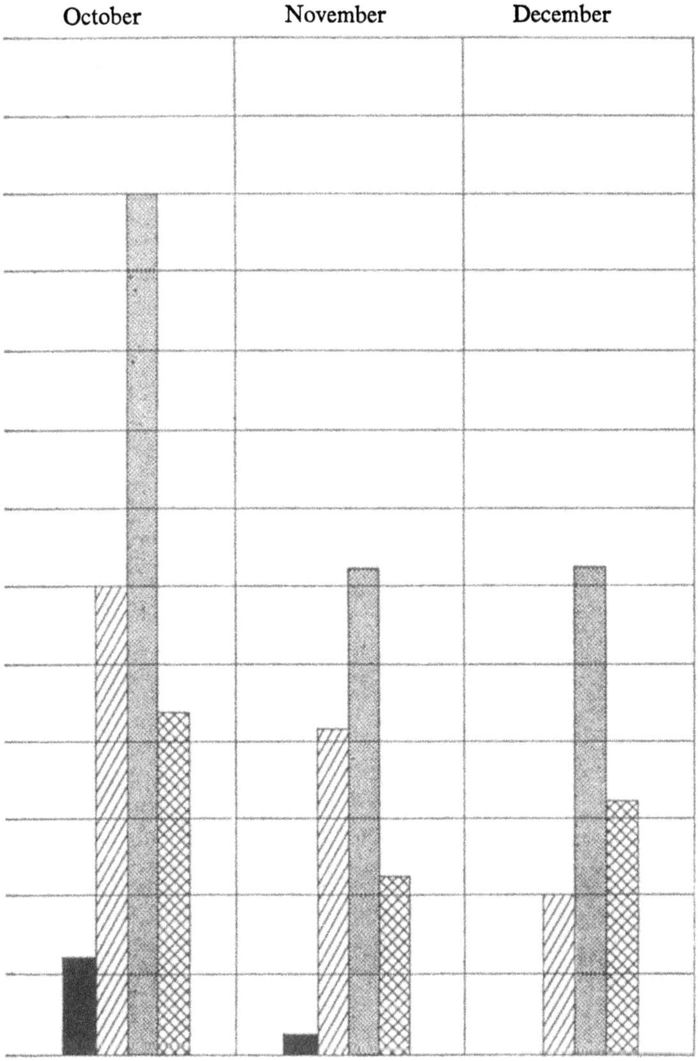

V. Results of Referendum Vote, *New York Post,* November 9, 1966

REVIEW BOARD SUMMARY

	YES (AGAINST BD.)	NO (FOR BD.)
Manhattan	168,391	234,485
The Bronx	235,310	128,084
Brooklyn	414,133	201,336
Queens	426,821	191,787
Richmond	63,083	12,800
Totals	1,307,738	768,492

"Yes" majority, 539,246.

VOTE ON REVIEW BOARD

MANHATTAN

A.D.	YES (AGAINST)	NO (FOR)
60	12,604	8,381
61	8,492	8,901
62	19,605	22,360
63	14,875	22,958
64	18,763	24,870
65	12,619	16,659
66	16,308	26,594
67	8,682	17,708
68	5,350	7,139
69	6,985	14,444
70	3,332	10,507
71	11,409	14,521
72	2,656	11,044
73	23,456	13,193
74	3,255	15,206
Totals	168,391	234,485

"No" majority, 66,094

BROOKLYN

A.D.	YES (AGAINST)	NO (FOR)
35	14,594	3,845
36	10,248	3,936
37	3,569	6,527
38	16,102	4,484
39	21,341	9,420
40	14,278	7,995
41	26,510	9,462
42	30,684	10,349
43	23,926	12,993
44	27,589	18,072
45	26,606	17,176
46	26,234	13,236
47	24,897	9,635
48	21,978	8,731
49	27,043	5,522
50	29,195	5,442
51	23,168	8,283
52	10,437	8,279
53	13,371	3,385
54	8,090	10,589
55	3,312	9,002
56	2,581	9,148
57	8,469	5,825
Totals	414,133	201,336

"Yes" majority, 212,797.

VOTE ON REVIEW BOARD

THE BRONX

A.D.	YES (AGAINST BD.)	NO (FOR BD.)
75	9,994	9,795
76	19,759	11,126
77	3,957	8,246
78	3,987	11,330
79	7,439	8,742
80	34,493	8,759
81	14,302	8,460
82	25,398	10,433
83	28,449	10,653
84	30,022	22,361
85	31,392	8,883
86	26,118	9,296
Totals	235,310	128,084

"Yes" majority, 107,226

RICHMOND

A.D.	YES (AGAINST BD.)	NO (FOR BD.)
58	35,420	6,609
59	27,663	6,191
Totals	63,083	12,800

"Yes" Majority, 50,283

QUEENS

A.D.	YES (AGAINST BD.)	NO (FOR BD.)
19	28,007	11,591
20	31,407	7,665
21	32,429	17,302
22	32,169	12,837
23	28,118	16,076
24	21,478	13,425
25	25,159	21,016
26	11,323	23,434
27	24,234	17,190
28	27,153	6,362
29	29,928	6,959
30	33,916	6,186
31	23,240	10,900
32	28,457	8,726
33	23,789	6,112
34	26,014	6,006
Totals	426,821	191,787

"Yes" majority, 235,034.

Bibliography

Clark, Kenneth B. *Dark Ghetto.* New York: Harper & Row, 1965.

Gellhorn, Walter. *When Americans Complain.* Cambridge, Massachusetts: Harvard University Press, 1966.

Goldstein, Joseph. *Police Policy Formulation: A Proposal for Improving Police Performance.* #65 Michigan Law Review. Ann Arbor, Michigan, 1967.

Gray, Ed. *The Big Blue Line.* New York: Coward-McCann, Inc., 1967.

Niederhoffer, Arthur. *Behind the Shield.* Garden City, New York: Doubleday & Co., Inc., 1967.

Skolnick, Jerome H. *Justice without Trial: Law Enforcement in Democratic Society.* New York: John Wiley & Sons, Inc., 1966.

SPECIAL REPORTS, PAMPHLETS, ARTICLES, BULLETINS, ETC.

Anderson, Stanley V. edited *Ombudsmen for American Government.* The American Assembly. Englewood Cliffs, New Jersey: Prentice-Hall, 1968.

Littman, Sol I. *The Policeman Looks at Himself.* Pamphlet. New York: Anti-Defamation League of B'nai B'rith, 1967.

Negroes and the Police. Editorial Research Reports. Washington, D.C., September 21, 1964.

Police Power and Citizens' Rights. American Civil Liberties Union. New York, 1966.

Report of the National Advisory Commission on Civil Disorders. New York: Bantam Books, Inc., 1968.

Report of the President's Commission on Law Enforcement and Administration of Justice. Washington: D.C. U.S. Printing Office, 1966.

"Civil Liberties in New York," A monthly bulletin of the New York Civil Liberties Union.

www.ingramcontent.com/pod-product-compliance
Ingram Content Group UK Ltd.
Pitfield, Milton Keynes, MK11 3LW, UK
UKHW020138290926
15471UKWH00003B/565